No Such Thing as a Bully
Shred a Label, Save a Child
Revised Version (Second Edition)

Bullyproofing Protection
for Parents and Children

Kelly Karius RSW

Copyright © 2011, 2022 by Karius and Associates

http://nosuchthingasabully.com

Revised Version (Second Edition)
   ISBN 978-0-9736831-4-1 (paperback)
   ISBN 978-0-9736831-6-5 (ebook)
   ISBN 978-0-9736831-2-7 (audio)

Cover Design by Cynthia Mikolas, Photo from fotolia.com

All definitions have been taken from Merriam-Webster online dictionary (https://www.merriam-webster.com/) unless otherwise noted.

Except for brief reviews, no part of this book may be reproduced in any form or by any means, electronic or mechanical, including photocopying, recording, or by any information storage and retrieval system, without the written permission of the publisher.

The publisher/author does not assume any responsibility for liability arising from any error or omission in this book, or from the use of any information contained in it.

The information contained within is for reference and education only and is not intended to be a substitute for professional assistance where necessary.

SHRED THE LABEL, SAVE A CHILD

NO SUCH THING AS A BULLY

BULLYPROOFING PROTECTION FOR PARENTS AND CHILDREN

Kelly Karius RSW

Note to Parents

This is lifetime material. You can start using it immediately, but the most important thing you must understand is that there is no end point to its use. In the best interests of your child, you will need to review it from time to time. As you learn and use these skills, and gain an understanding of the problem of bullying, you will be able to teach your child.

This material, while introduced lesson by lesson, will show up in everyday situations. YOU are the one who will see the teachable moments in those everyday situations. YOU are the only one who can teach your child through them. After all, YOU are your child's major influence. Guidance happens daily and when you know the material well—and live it—you are going to be able to teach it successfully.

Bullyproofing doesn't just mean protecting your child from having bully actions used against them. It also means preventing your child from using bully actions; it means raising a child who is strong enough to stop bully actions when they are seen. A little effort on your part will go a long way toward bullyproofing your child and helping him to become an adult who will make a difference in the world.

This book will help you to discuss these issues with your child and you will be guided to watch your own reactions. Use the modules to build your relationship and to understand your child's life. It will be time well spent.

Contents

Note to Parents   5
Introduction   9

PART 1: General Information/Background

Rationale   13
Goals for Parents   14
Kelly's Story   15
Definitions   18
Recognizing the Signs   20
Approaching Your Child   22
Risk Assessment   24
Levels of Intervention   25
When An Influential Adult Is Using Bully Actions   29
"Screen Time" and Bullying   30
Recognizing the Frames of Reference   31
Children Experiencing Bullying   33
Predicting Violent Behavior   34
Bullying Outcomes   36
The Bullying Spiral   37
Real Life School Bullying   38
When Your Child is Using Bully Actions   41
When Your Child is Using Victim Responses   42
When Your Child is a Bystander   43
Self Esteem   44
Teaching Points for Your Child   45
Role-Playing   47
Defining the Problem   48
Brainstorming   50
Pledging   52
Goals   53
Self-Assessment of Your Own Communication Style   54

PART 2: Protection Lessons for Parents and Children

Protection One: Conflict vs. Bullying	59
Protection Two: Feelings	62
Protection Three: Fight, Flight, or Freeze	65
Protection Four: Important Ideas	67
Protection Five: The Bullying Spiral	71
Protection Six: Working Through Harm	74
Protection Seven: How You Act	78
Protection Eight: Friendship Skills	82
Protection Nine: Bill of Rights and Responsibilities	87
Protection Ten: Bully Actions and Victim Responses	90
Protection Eleven: Saying No	98
Protection Twelve: "I" Sentences	102
Protection Thirteen: Always and Never	106
Protection Fourteen: Questions	107
Protection Fifteen: Tone of Voice	109
Protection Sixteen: Body Language	111
Protection Seventeen: Thinking	114
Protection Eighteen: Inaccurate Thinking	115
Protection Nineteen: Automatic Thoughts	121
Protection Twenty: Balanced Thinking	125
Protection Twenty-One: The Anxiety Equation	130
Protection Twenty-Two: Taking Care of Yourself	134
Protection Twenty-Three: Lucky or Unlucky	135
Protection Twenty-Four: Control	138
Protection Twenty-Five: Affirmations	140
Plans to Review	143
References	145
Contacts for No Such Thing as a Bully®	148

Introduction

The day your baby arrives, you discover more emotions than you ever thought you could have. You lovingly wrap, feed and change your precious bundle. As your child grows you spend time wondering, worrying, childproofing, protecting. You'd give up your life to protect that precious child. You don't want your child to be hurt by his own actions, any more than you want him to be hurt by someone else.

Imagine you're the parent of an active and outgoing 7-year-old boy. One day your precious little man seems "off." You can't put your finger on it, but he's just not his usual happy self. You ask what's wrong. "Nothing, I'm okay," he says. You are still concerned.

Time moves on.

Another day, you see a bad bruise on his leg and hip. "We were playing dodgeball," he explains. "Boys," you might say, and ruffle his hair.

Time moves on.

Your son develops a stomachache that lasts for two days. The trouble is unclear. You tell him that sometimes, when people are upset, they actually feel physical pain; you ask if anything is bothering him; he starts to cry.

It turns out that negative relationships have been created in the school and your son doesn't know how to handle them. Bigger boys have been picking on him. He's been pushed down, called names, and had his homework taken from him. He's trying to be a sport about it, laughing along or just trying to avoid them, but they scare him. Lately he has felt afraid to go to school, afraid to tell anyone—even you, his parents—how he's feeling. He begs you not to go to the school.

Now what?

As this happens, another scene plays out in another home. A parent gets a call about a child who is using bully actions against another child; a parent hears a story about an argument and doesn't know how to handle it.

Maybe a parent knows exactly where the bullying behavior is coming from but doesn't have the resources or knowledge to stop it.

This familiar scene is played out in households across the nation. It involves boys and girls of all ages. It leaves parents and children scared and confused. School organizations feel helpless. Sometimes the bullying spreads to the internet so that even in his own home a child cannot avoid his tormentors.

This book is for parents on both sides. Sometimes you are angered by each other. You have different perspectives and you think you have different goals. But you don't. You aren't on different teams. Your children all need the same life skills to move them forward and teach them different and more positive ways of interacting with others.

You need the tools to examine your own thinking and behavior so you can transfer those skills to your children. This version of **No Such Thing as a Bully** will teach you how to work with your children to overcome bully actions.

PART 1
General Information/Background

Rationale

This book will not use the terms "bully" and "victim." These more common labels have been replaced with "bully actions" and "victim responses." Every person has the capacity to use both types of behavior in certain situations and with certain individuals.

Telling a child that they are a victim or a bully increases the chance the behavior will continue. It puts the child into a box. Once we see a child by a label we may miss everything else that child can be.

Talking about bullies and victims also minimizes the role of the bystander. We believe it is important for adult role models to check in with their own behavior. Every child needs a skill set that will keep them mentally healthy and teach them how to respond. Adults must be aware of the responses they are modeling for the children around them. Habits can be changed.

Childhood provides an abundance of teaching opportunities to help children make positive choices about how they will communicate, build their self-concept and build relationships with the people around them. We believe actions and responses can be changed. Children who can overcome bullying are well-positioned to navigate conflict in their adult lives. It is our responsibility to teach them how.

Goals for Parents

- Understand the dynamics and outcomes of bullying.

- Move from seeing your child as a bully or a victim to understanding that these are patterns of behavior that can be changed.

- Learn how to strengthen bystander children.

- Learn to use the tools provided here, that will assist with prevention and intervention in bullying situations.

- Gain tools to change thinking patterns, increase self-confidence, and be able to transfer that knowledge to your children.

- Use the ideas and tools provided to approach bullying situations.

Kelly's Story

Throughout my life, I have learned that I can make conscious changes to my own behavior. I have seen that the way I act and react affects the responses of those around me in every situation. As a result, I believe that bullying can be controlled—person by person, action by action.

The pendulum swung for me as I learned how to communicate properly and how to make things happen. I moved from being bullied to bullying to fighting bullying.

In my home, "tough" was a value. I was a gentle soul and had trouble acclimating to that. My dad had trouble disciplining me because I cried too easily. I well remember the phrase, "Stop crying or I'll give you something to cry about!" I remember a lot of horseplay between my two brothers, but I was treated differently. Well, except for that one time when I was a baby and they tried to put me in the dryer. The most traumatic physical things that I experienced were occasional spankings—mostly a quick backhand on my butt from my mom as I was going by—and being tickled until I almost peed my pants.

I wasn't competitive either. I had trouble understanding why they only used one puck for hockey when there was a whole pail of pucks in the scorekeeper's box. Why were they all fighting about one silly puck when there was enough for everyone?

I was always the big kid in elementary school. I recall thinking that I was fat, but when I look back at pictures it's clear that I wasn't. Still, I was taller and broader than all the other girls in the class. That's OK when you're a boy; not so much when you're a girl. I remember being weighed in class, and all our weights being written on the chalkboard. I was the first one to get past a hundred pounds in grade 5, making the sting of my hated nickname—Kelly Jelly Smelly Belly—even worse. I remember social isolation from girls who, now as women, probably feel terrible about some of their actions. I recall two of my friends and myself all wearing white on the same day in school. We were called clouds, and the others stopped talking to us for a few days. How very random is that? The three of us continue to be friends.

I've reconnected with some of the other girls. Some may even read this and recognize themselves and be sad about their actions. I don't write this to make anyone sad. We were unregulated. Bullying wasn't talked about, yet it existed with all the same symptoms we see now. The girls and boys I felt bullied by are now women and men. I still know most of them, and I like them. They are not the same people they were—nor am I.

Looking back to middle school makes me understand that through all of this, my self-concept was completely out-of-whack. I wasn't sure who I was, and the parts of me that I was sure about I saw as negative. I was looking for my self-concept in the comments of others.

In middle school I started to buy into the idea of "tough" as a value. Tough made people scared of me. No one called me Kelly Jelly Smelly Belly anymore. A new Kelly emerged: she always wore a jean jacket, smoked at school and beat up a boy in the boy's bathroom when he was going to tell.

Middle School Kelly lipped off to teachers; she played Juice Newton's Playing with the Queen of Hearts from her locker while O Canada! was on the school speakers. This Kelly spent a bit of time in the Principal's office.

My heart was still good. I wanted to help people. I knew there were things I was doing that were wrong, but I was the tough class clown and I wasn't willing to sacrifice that for Kelly Jelly Smelly Belly. My new nickname was Orv. I was one of a few in the school that were honored with our opposite parent's name as a nickname. It meant we were accepted to some extent. I apologize to those I hurt in middle school. (You know who you are.) And there may be some people that I've hurt without even knowing. I apologize for that too.

In high school, I found an even keel, becoming the girl that most people liked and hardly anyone teased. There was no longer need for the misplaced, ill-fitting, tough persona that I had carried. I learned the freedom of helping others, the social connection of listening and being a good friend. I am honored to have many lifetime friendships with people from all parts of my school years.

For me, there was an innate sense of right and wrong, an empathy for others that kept me from heading too far into the bullying path. Underneath my journey to that path, and my sense of victimization in school, was an inaccurate belief that I wasn't good enough; that somehow, girls had to be a certain weight and have a certain look in order to have value. If we couldn't achieve those things naturally, then we acted in ways that we perceived would give us value.

Training as a social worker brought exposure to families and children who were struggling with bullying issues on an ongoing basis. This solidified my desire to not only find that even keel, but to advocate for change. Big change. The world needs to learn to work with its children, through childhood and beyond, to remind them that they are who they are and they have value just because they exist. Children must be told they are beautiful, inside and out. Differences must be noted and celebrated without becoming a focus. Social media myths must be addressed. Children must understand that they don't have to look like supermodels or avatars. They are who they are and they are blessed and valued. They must be shown that over and over.

We don't create their journey, but we do contribute. As adults, we must understand these things about ourselves as well, then we must transfer them to our children.

Definitions

High Bullying Value (HBV) Frame of Reference =	desire to hurt + superior power/ enjoyment + desire for control/ contempt
ACTION =	hurtful + repeated
High Victim Response (HVR) Frame of Reference =	vulnerability + sense of oppression/ unjust treatment

Bullying can thus be described in equation form (Rigby):

Bullying = HBV + ACTION + HVR

Types of bully actions include:

- **Physical:** striking another person; damaging or stealing another person's property
- **Verbal:** name-calling, teasing, humiliating, or threatening
- **Social:** excluding others, spreading rumors, humiliation, interference in relationships
- **Cyber/Electronic:** verbal and/or social bullying via Internet or phone (Canadian Public Health Association)
- **Sexual:** physical or verbal actions relating to one's sexual being or sexuality

The High Bullying Value (HBV) Frame of Reference contains the aspects of having a desire to hurt, using harmful actions to create a sense of superiority, and trying to control situations and people around them.

When the HBV Frame of Reference is combined with hurtful and repeated action against someone who carries or may be prone to a High Victim Response (HVR) Frame of Reference, a bullying situation takes place. Someone who is prone to an HVR Frame of Reference has a sense of vulnerability and helplessness. They feel incapable of protecting themselves from a person with an HBV Frame of Reference. They react in fear to the illusion of the sense of power and control that accompanies an HBV Frame of Reference.

We all have the capacity to use bully actions in particular situations and under certain conditions, but few of us will identify ourselves as bullies. For this reason, the phrases "High Bullying Value Frame of Reference" and "High Victim Response Frame of Reference" are used here, rather than the labelling words bully and victim. No one needs to be categorized as either a full-time bully or a full-time victim. Rather, we wish to provide ways to assess which behaviors and attitudes contribute to the syndrome of bullying. Eliminating these actions and attitudes works toward eliminating the syndrome of bullying rather than eliminating or denigrating people.

The definition illustrates a fundamental power imbalance. When the power between people is unbalanced bully actions can escalate to a bullying situation.

Bystander behavior becomes a bully action when it supports the bully actions of another. Bystanders who feel the same emotions and intentions as the person using the bully actions are actually active supporters, and they are using bully actions as well. Some bystanders do not feel the contempt, control, desire to hurt, and enjoyment required to define bullying, but they may not stand up in defense of others because of fear, lack of self-confidence, or lack of knowledge about what to do.

Ultimately, children using any of these three behaviors—bully actions, victim responses, and bystander behaviors—need skills to help them positively build their self-concept, balance their thinking, increase their self-confidence, gain empathy and understanding, and learn superior communication skills.

Recognizing the Signs

Children who are experiencing bullying might:
- be afraid of how they will get to school
- indicate they would like to make changes to their schedule
- become afraid to go to school entirely
- have mysterious and undiagnosed pains or illness
- experience lower grades and suffer in their schoolwork
- appear less confident
- withdraw and/or become anxious
- become aggressive with other children
- have changes in appetite
- not fully explain any bruises, cuts, or scratches
- have property go missing or be ruined
- give excuses that don't make sense
- act secretively and/or begin stealing
- experience negative mood changes after interacting online or by cell phone

Children who are bullying and using bully actions might:
- talk negatively and derogatorily about some of their peers
- freely use negative labels contemptuously in conversation
- portray themselves as a victim when their behavior is confronted
- blame the other child
- not see the need to apologize for their behavior
- show contempt for other children
- act differently in front of adults than in front of peers

- have low levels of empathy
- have extremely high or extremely low self-esteem
- have previously experienced bully actions against themselves
- have a role model who acts aggressively

Children who are bystanders might:
- try to distance themselves from the actions
- be fearful of the child using bully actions
- try to stay friends with the child using bully actions
- talk about conflict between their peers
- try to figure out how to handle the situation without adult intervention
- be afraid of the reaction of the child using bully actions if they stand up for another child
- be open to strong leadership in the area of bullying prevention and intervention
- be well placed to utilize bullyproofing tools in their schools and communities

Approaching Your Child

If you see any of these symptoms, it is crucial for you to talk to your child. Important points when broaching the subject:

1. Try not to make a big deal of the approach, especially with older children. Make use of a shared activity or driving time together to explore how your child's peer friendships and relationships are going. Be careful not to be judgmental.

2. Even if you are not concerned that your child is experiencing difficulties, discussing relationships is good practice. Starting early to talk about peer relationships sets the scene for talking about them in later years, when such conversations tend to become more difficult.

3. If your child does not disclose any problem, yet you are still concerned, focus on what you have seen. Tell your child about the changes you've noticed in them or other things you are noticing and ask about the cause. Give details of what can be seen from the outside. Ask directly if your child is experiencing or using bully actions or being exposed to bullying at school. Assure your child that you can work together to solve the problem.

4. Be careful not to create a problem where one did not exist before. A child may be experiencing bully actions, but if they are able to handle the situation on their own, with your coaching, they begin to gain their own life experience.
    Remember that conflict is part of a child's life, just as it is part of an adult's life. Conflict in childhood is the training ground for managing conflict well as an adult. It is important to understand the distinction between conflict and bullying and discern when to step in as a parent.
    When a parent takes over for a child, rather than coaching the child to handle their own small conflicts, opportunities for learning are missed. When a parent minimizes conflict without coaching them, learning opportunities are also missed. We must acknowledge the conflict in our children's lives and distinguish between

what they can handle on their own and when they need adults to intervene. When a situation is bullying and a parent intervenes, it must be done in a way that is proactive, positive, and resolution-focused.

5. If you are reacting strongly as a parent, examine your reaction. Were you bullied in school? Are you being bullied now? We tend to react strongly to situations that we connect with emotionally. In a bullying situation, it is not helpful to your child for you to overreact. Plan your follow-up actions well, and clearly understand why you are taking your chosen steps.

6. Before approaching the school, do a risk assessment. Does your child feel he is in grave and immediate danger? If so, it is necessary to take action quickly. Don't be afraid to pull a child out of school until you figure out the situation, particularly in cases that have already become severe.

Use the following questions and levels of intervention to determine your child's levels of risk and the appropriate course of action.

Risk Assessment

A risk assessment includes the following steps:

STEP 1: Evaluate the possibility of harm.

STEP 2: Evaluate current safety plans.

STEP 3: Evaluate effects.

STEP 4: Determine the need for intervention.

1. What are the levels of bully actions that my child is experiencing? Rate each type of bullying (physical, verbal, sexual, cyber, social) on a scale of 1 to 10, 1 being not at all and 10 being very severe.

2. What supports are in place in the school setting that provide safety for my child? Consider: school culture, school policy, child's friendships, adult involvement in the school.

3. How is my child being affected? Using the list of effects in the "Recognizing the Signs" section (page 19), note the signs you are seeing in your child. Take note of any other signs you observe.

If you discover high numbers in question one, low supports in question two, and many effects in question three, then you'll know that you likely need to use several scales of intervention.

A combination of medium numbers in question one, consistent clear safety plans, and lower effects, lets you know that you need to provide intervention at the level of your child.

This is not a scientific tool; rather, it is intended to provide a framework that facilitates your ability to mindfully determine your next steps.

Levels of Intervention

Level 1: Intervention with child

Intervening directly with your child means teaching your child how to manage a bullying situation directly, through life skills, communication skills and tools that help to manage thinking and behavior.

Children using bully actions and children using victim responses both need the same skills. They may require different examples and different ways to understand the patterns of behavior, but the skills are the same.

In the second part of this book, you will learn the essential knowledge for managing both bully actions and victim responses. You will also learn how to transfer that knowledge to your children, regardless of how they are reacting.

Level 2: Intervention with other parents/children

Generally speaking, this is a step that needs to be taken very carefully. It is a good idea to lower your defenses prior to approaching the other parents. People will have a fight, flight, or freeze reaction if they are approached aggressively—and sometimes even if they are approached calmly. You must begin the conversation feeling that you are on the same team. Resolution involves moving from "me-against-you to us-against-the-problem" (Dana, 76) Another parent's response is going to be much more receptive if you are seeking solutions rather than approaching the situation with blame. If you are in the middle of a situation right now, and you feel like this type of perspective is an impossibility, then take the time to learn the skills in this book, as you make a decision about your approach. Keep in mind that it is rare for an aggressive approach to have a positive outcome.

Decide ahead of time what you wish to achieve by speaking with the other parent(s). Are you:

- trying to find out more information about the situation?
- making them aware of their own child's behavior?
- making them aware of your child's reaction?
- hoping to come up with a collaborative solution?

If a primary reason for talking with the other child's parent is to voice your anger or give them what you feel they 'deserve,' reconsider. It is essential that your intention is to assist in resolving the issue peacefully, or your involvement can potentially increase the problems. Do not involve children in this process at the outset. Children should only be involved if they feel safe and if both sets of parents are working toward a collaborative resolution. This resolution needs to involve apologizing for bully actions and moving forward in a way that has positive, long-term effects for the children involved.

It is possible that this intervention is more common for parents who find that their child is experiencing bully actions against them; however, if you want to become truly proactive about managing bullying, then you must also examine your child's behavior toward others.

If you say to yourself, "My child would never hurt another child," have another look. There is a culture of hurt out there for children and it is very difficult for children to be able to stay out of it—even those that are seen as 'good' children. Keep your eyes open.

Level 3: Intervention with schools

Again, be sure your approach is one that assures the school administration you are on their side. They are not your enemy. If your approach treats them like the enemy, they will not respond as well as you want them to and you may harm future relationships with them.

Let the school know what you are doing at home to work on solving the problem. If the school feels that you are simply throwing it in their lap, they will not be so receptive to taking responsibility.

Be active in the school: get on the PTA committee; stay in touch with your child's teacher; provide supervision at the school whenever you can; in a friendly, natural way, get to know children who are using bully actions.

All adults need to be willing to accept responsibility for assisting with management in an environment where bully actions can take place.

For the child using either victim responses or bully actions, the intervention at the school level is the same.

Remember that neither child is your enemy. Both children involved are exactly that—children.

Talk to your child's teacher about ways your child can be encouraged to become more assertive in school. Ask your school if they have—or are willing to arrange—a training program, using The **No Such Thing as a Bully** System. The material for schools is written to be used with groups of children in or out of the classroom.

Stay aware of your child's perception of safety, if they have experienced bully actions, and believe them if they tell you they are still afraid. Talk with the school counselor about your child's adaptation, and find out how the counselor is helping, or can help.

As you look for ways to be involved in the school in informal and supervisory capacities—whether your child is using bully actions or victim responses—encourage your school to use a system of restitution (fixing the problem), resolution (figuring out a way to keep it from happening again), and reconciliation (finding ways to heal with the person one has harmed).

Level 4: Intervention with systems

If you have approached the school and have not received a response that moves the situation toward resolution, you may choose to go a step higher and approach a school board or administration system.

If you decide to take this next step, do your research. Children are particularly at risk in schools that deny bullying problems, lack effective policies and procedures to address bullying, allow the development of (and even appear to support) a culture of regimented cliques that use bully actions, and have adults who avoid seeing and/or addressing bully actions.

Approach the organization with an awareness of their policies and procedures regarding bullying. Ask for a copy of the school and/or school division bullying policy. Look for others who have already done the research. There may be a group of concerned parents you can join with, rather than undertaking a system-change battle on your own. Think about who your support people are, and how they can help. Remember—the system generally holds more power than a disgruntled parent—if your approach is too aggressive, it may be ignored or minimized. Approach the people who have a stake in the system with feasible solutions rather than simply throwing your problem at them.

We suggest you explore the option of a **No Such Thing as a Bully** Community Immersion, which involves intensive teaching from a Certified Facilitator, or present the idea of people in your community becoming certified in effective tools to strengthen youth and parents. This will provide a change to the fundamental systems that are creating a problem. You can find more information at http://nosuchthingasabully.com.

When An Influential Adult Is Using Bully Actions

This is one of the most difficult situations. It must be approached with a great deal of assertive behavior. The adult must be approached in a way that helps him or her to understand the child's perceptions. It is likely that the adult is not going to immediately say, "Oh, hey, yeah, I AM a bully!" but they may be able to say, "Okay, I can see how that may have come across wrong."

Adults often engage in bully actions. This work is intended to change their skill level in terms of assertive approaches. It is to give them skills they didn't have and help them more fully understand the skills they already have. Children benefit most when the adults teaching them understand how to live with flexible, but clear, assertive boundaries. School policies and staff must also reflect assertive and thoughtful principles and actions.

If you suspect your child is being bullied by an adult, it is important to gather information from your child about what they perceive is happening. As your child gets older, this gets easier. Present the information to the adult as the child's perception, then ask the adult to explain the situation from their point of view. You may not receive satisfactory answers immediately, but it is important then to watch the follow up behavior. Sometimes simply challenging a behavior is enough to remove it.

If that is ineffective, and if the adult is a teacher, you may have to extend involvement to the principal. If this is the route you decide to take, be sure your information is solid and well documented. You may choose to check options for changing primary classrooms or, if the situation remains unresolved, you may even consider changing schools.

People in authority occasionally use their power in a bullying manner. When this happens, you must be prepared to consciously evaluate the situation. Without flying off the handle, take steps to improve your child's situation, providing protection if necessary.

"Screen Time" and Bullying

While the research linking aggressive behavior in children to violent games and videos is not conclusive, as parents we know that children are affected by the games they play.

Take a moment right now to think about the childhood games YOU played. I'll bet you can name them and attach memories to them. You remember who you were playing them with, and you remember how they made you feel.

Now, picture the 11-year-old in his room playing Call of Duty. All of his friends have it, mom didn't really LOOK at it, and he REALLY wanted it. He immerses himself in war. He throws out curses. He shoots people. Sometimes he plays with friends. Sometimes he plays with "Lintmuffin," someone he met online.

He moves from playing COD with Lintmuffin and his friends to checking out his social media accounts. He takes a few pictures of himself, checks out a cruel fake page a couple of girls made about another girl, leaves a nasty comment.

Hopefully, in there somewhere, he is also playing a healthy game of football, or spending time with his mom and dad, but he may not be. It is up to you to screen your child's games, making sure they are appropriate, limiting the amount of time spent in this way. Life is all about balance.

Some things to watch for include:

- A child trying to deny your access to their computer or gaming systems.

- A child whose mood changes after being on the computer or checking their cell phone.

- A child who does not want their parents involved in any of the social media sites they use.

The more unsupervised and unquestioned time a child spends in front of an interactive screen, the more susceptible they become to cyberbully actions and victim responses. Monitor your child's use of electronics carefully—computer, cell phone, gaming systems–and educate yourself about the danger. Seek out a protection app to install on your child's first phone. Such a safety application will connect you with your child's social media pages and cell phone, sending you alerts as you choose.

Recognizing the Frames of Reference

Keep in mind that those using these frames of reference defy stereotypes.

Characteristics

High Bullying Value Frame of Reference	High Victim Response Frame of Reference
• Actions are impulsive and aggressive • Difficulty in regulating mood and high frustration levels • Actions may involve breaking the law • Remorse does not follow actions, lack of empathy • May be supported in their actions by peers and even by family • Directs blame at others rather than at self • Underdeveloped relational problem-solving skills • May be a response to authoritarian or inconsistent parenting • May be unskilled in evaluating their own behavior	• Actions are anxious, insecure or shy • May present as cautious, lacking confidence, passive • Few peer friends and supporters • May present as different from others in some way • Offers "entertaining" reactions • Directs blame at self • May feel discouraged about making any change in their situation • May be afraid to ask for adult help, fearing that "tattling" will make the situation worse • May be too embarrassed and/or humiliated to ask for help.

Individuals can counteract the characteristics

High Bullying Value Frame of Reference	High Victim Response Frame of Reference
• Learn limits • Understand and accept responsibility for actions and consequences • Control the fight, flight, or freeze response • Develop problem-solving skills • Express emotions and communicate positively • Learn understanding and empathy • Be reinforced for expressing emotions positively • Be given an opportunity to appropriately resolve the issue	• Find social support in a safe setting • Learn and grow in a safe setting • Take pride in differences • Develop assertive skills, including speech, attitude, and body language • Receive direct coaching in replying to bully actions • Be safely involved in the consequences of bullying

The descriptions of the Frames of Reference don't change appreciably, whatever form the bullying may take: physical, verbal, social, cyber/electronic, sexual.

Bystanders play an extremely important role. It has been shown that the quickest way for bullying to stop is for bystanders to step up in defense of the child who is experiencing bully actions.

Every child is affected by bullying, if not directly, then as a bystander. Every child needs to be taught to identify and confront bully actions. They need to understand and appreciate differences and understand the potentially tragic effects of bullying.

Even if a child is not using or experiencing bully actions, approach them with this information from a bystander point of view. The bystander has the most important role in this syndrome, and our youth must be educated enough to be strong bystanders.

Children Experiencing Bullying

Symptom	Reasons
Lack of interest in school or refusal to go to school.	Fear, logical response, avoidance of bully actions.
Taking an unusual route to school.	Fear, logical response, avoidance of bully actions.
Demonstrating a negative mood change after receiving a phone call or email.	Sense of shame in talking about ugly calls.
Drop in grades	Lowered concentration, focus is on avoiding the bully action, or sometimes plotting revenge.
Withdrawal from family activities	Carrying a sense of humiliation and shame, fear of disclosure.
Withdrawal from peer activities	Humiliation and shame, fear of being in unprotected regions
Extreme after-school hunger	Symptomatic of lunch or lunch money extortion
Stealing or asking for money more than usual	Symptomatic of extortion
Using the bathroom immediately at home	May indicate the bathroom at school is an unsafe place.

Predicting Violent Behavior

It is difficult to predict violent human behavior. We are an unpredictable species. Many can go through extremely traumatic ongoing incidents of violence and bullying and overcome them, while still living with the results. Other children may deal with what adults perceive as only a slight amount of violence and/or bullying before turning to violent behavior themselves. How the adults around them react and encourage them to react to the bullying issues they experience matters as well.

Indicators of escalated teen violence (de Becker):

- Alcohol and drug abuse
- Addiction to media products
- Aimlessness (constantly changing goals and ambitions, unrealistic expectations, and lack of perseverance and self-discipline to reach the goals).
- Fascination with weapons
- Experience with guns
- Access to guns
- Sullen, angry, depressed
- Seeking status and worth through violence
- Threats (of violence or suicide)
- Chronic anger
- Rejection/humiliation
- Media Provocation: Widely publicized major acts of violence can stimulate people who identify with the perpetrators and the attention they receive.

Seven key abilities people must have to effectively manage life (Goleman):

- self-motivation
- persistence against frustration
- delaying gratification
- mood regulation
- hope
- empathy
- impulse control

Essentially, many of these basic skills are untaught, except by example. And when a child is experiencing bully actions against him, it becomes difficult to manage the situation if he has not developed these basic skills. These are the skills that keep our children alive and well!

The child without motivation cannot develop the energy to see the future, never mind creating it. The child that cannot persist against frustration is not able to learn difficult concepts or change negative behaviors. The child who cannot delay gratification cannot see tomorrow clearly. The child who cannot regulate his moods is unable to attach thought to emotion and logically examine and change moods and circumstances.

The child who is unable to hope becomes depressed and often suicidal. The child who is unable to empathize turns to the same violence and anger that they are experiencing, at times taking great satisfaction and power in creating a new, angry, violent energy around themselves. Children unable to control their impulses have not learned to use forward thinking patterns to assess life.

This book actively teaches those skills to adults, and then teaches adults how to actively teach the skills to their children.

Bullying Outcomes

We know (many of us from personal experience) that the child bullied in school is not likely to feel safe. If a child is beaten up and/or terrorized, the child will spend the rest of the school year walking home along a different route to avoid another beating or humiliation. Many children feel they must spend recess time in the close vicinity of a teacher. Many children have trouble making friends, because other children—potential friends—don't want to risk becoming a target of bullying themselves. Those who define themselves or are defined as a victim feel that they are unable to change or adjust their situation. They feel they must wait for some external change (e.g., a change in schools because of passing a grade) or some other outside force (e.g., direct intervention of an adult).

Consider these after-effects in those who have been exposed to bullying by classmates:

- Decline in quality of schoolwork

- Problems with attendance

- Difficulty sleeping at night—perhaps including nightmares—leading to school days full of exhaustion and lethargy for the child.

- Avoidance of certain areas of the school, especially bathrooms, showers, gym—places where adults are frequently absent.

This leads to decreased performance in school and the loss of opportunity to make good friends and engage in lasting hobbies. The long-term effects can be loss of educational and/or employment opportunities. The loss of self-esteem and loss of opportunity can lead those experiencing a High Victim Response Frame of Reference to become offenders themselves, and sometimes even to attempt or complete suicide or revenge.

The Bullying Spiral

The Spiral indicates the cycle that is built when bullying actions are not addressed in a straight forward manner. One person is approached by another person. If one person has learned to control by power, the grooming pattern includes testing; How will this person react to me? The teasing, threats and/or harmful actions continue and accelerate as long as the situation is not addressed and the victim responses continue. Bystanders play an important role in determining if the situation will escalate or be derailed. The players are likely to be characterized as bully and victim. The person using victim responses comes to see themselves as helpless. The person using bully actions learns that power works to get their own way. The "victim" may, at some point, lash out with a bully action and may then be characterized as a bully instead of a victim. Ultimately, both parties may experience destruction.

We will talk more about The Bullying Spiral in Protection 5 on page 71.

Real Life School Bullying

Dawn-Marie Wesley

By November 10, 2000, Dawn-Marie Wesley, 14, of Mission BC had been dealing with bullying from several girls for many months. The situation met the definition of bullying as provided on pages 17 and 90. There had been a breakdown of friendships in her peer group, resulting in several girls bullying Dawn-Marie. Rumors were spread about Dawn-Marie. Threats were made. Dawn-Marie felt it was necessary to speak to her school counselor daily and she was always sure not to walk home from school by herself. On the evening of November 10th, one of the girls yelled at her over the phone, "You are f***ing dead!"

Bystanders were co-opted into the group and assisted in the harassment or were silent about it. Only two of Dawn-Marie's friends tried to intervene.

Dawn-Marie was depressed and tired and scared. She must have felt she had nowhere to turn. Believing that the girls were going to kill her or hurt her, she wrote in her suicide note that she had been threatened by bullies and believed death was her only escape. She said she was depressed and couldn't tell anyone about the abuse because the girls tormenting her would get suspended and then the situation would only get worse. One girl, who witnessed one of the girls threatening to kill Dawn-Marie, said, "I would have stopped it if I could, but it happened so fast."

Dawn-Marie used her dog's leash to hang herself in her bedroom, and was later found by her 13-year-old brother. Two girls were charged for uttering threats. One of the girls was additionally charged with criminal harassment. The girl with a single charge was acquitted. The girl with two charges was convicted. The offenders cannot be named because of the Young Offenders Act.

The defense argued that the bullying actions were normal schoolyard behavior and stated the teens never intended or planned to kill Dawn-Marie. The prosecution conceded that there may not have been intent to kill; however, the accused terrorized Dawn-Marie and that, in itself, is criminal behavior. This was an issue of bullying, the first of its kind to be tried in Canada.

According to B.C. Provincial Court Judge Jill Rounthwaite the question was narrow and legal:

> "When do school yard taunts cross over the line to become a criminal offence of threatening death or bodily harm? When does a teenager's annoying behavior toward a fellow student amount to an offence of criminal harassment?" (*The Province*)

These are the questions to which she applied the law. Judge Rounthwaite said that it was clear that one of the accused had bullied Wesley repeatedly, giving the victim reason to fear for her life. She noted that the bystanders took part in adding "to the power of the bully by not intervening." The second girl sentenced had taken part in the final phone call, however there was no evidence the girl had broken the law.

Cindy Wesley, mother of Dawn Marie, requested that the convicted girl be sentenced using an aboriginal sentencing circle. She wanted to honor the memory of her daughter's partial aboriginal history, as well as that of the offender. All parties to the action agreed. Dawn-Marie's mom wanted a chance to speak with the teenager and her family.

During the sentencing circle the teen took the ceremonial eagle feather twice and tried to speak. She broke down each time and was urged by Cindy Wesley to try again. The teen was ultimately able to apologize. The offender's family hopes the case will keep other girls from making the same mistake. They hope that the sentencing circle process will set the offender on the right track.

The offender received 18 months' probation with terms including no use of alcohol or drugs, random drug testing, counseling and anger management and a prohibition on cell phone use. She needed to write a 750-word essay on bullying and complete 20 hours of community service as well.

A documentary has been made called "Rats & Bullies", which tells Dawn-Marie's story and explores the unique characteristics of female bullying while offering methods of bullying prevention.

Emmet Fralick

In April of 2002, in Halifax, Emmet Fralick, a 14-year-old grade 9 student, couldn't take the abuse anymore. Emmet was being harassed by peers at his school.

A group of teenagers, led by a 15-year-old girl, made demands on Emmet, including giving them up to $80 each day. When Emmet couldn't come up with the money, he was put in a circle and forced to choose which one of his peers would beat him up that day. He was punched, kicked, burned with cigarettes and forced to eat dog feces. He received a broken nose, black eyes, and a broken thumb through these abuses.

Emmet was afraid to tell those who cared what was happening. He would lie about his bruises or hide them. He sold everything he owned to try to pay the offenders. He was caught shoplifting as he was attempting to steal items he could sell to get the money. Emmet's friends knew what he was experiencing and would sometimes give him money, but all the children were too afraid to tell an adult what was happening.

Bullying continued in the school after Fralick committed suicide, but students began to ask for more help. Students said, "Because this whole thing happened, no one's going to take anything from anyone anymore" and "If anything good came out of the suicide, it was the fact that it brought the problem forward."

Emmet Fralick's parents urge other parents to be involved in their children's lives and to try to be aware of what's happening for their children.

> Lois Fralic [Emmet's mom] says she knew her son was troubled, but had no idea what he was really up against because of the strong code of silence among teenagers. She has this advice for other parents.
>
> "Talk to your children, love your children, hug your children, if they are begging you not to get involved, please get involved." (CBC News)

One girl in this case was charged with extortion, assault, and threat to cause bodily harm. She was sentenced to one year in youth jail. The same girl has pleaded guilty to three other charges stemming from another case of bullying.

When Your Child is Using Bully Actions

When you see or hear that your child is using bully actions with other children, you must create expectations that will stop the behavior, and examine your own actions.

1. Do you laugh at or mock others in your child's presence—even in what might seem like small ways to you?
2. Do you make derogatory jokes that others sometimes don't appreciate?
3. Do you engage in, or talk about physical violence as a resolution tactic?
4. Do you engage in, or talk about revenge tactics?
5. Do you display disrespect for other people?
6. Do you send messages to your child that fighting means you are strong or tough?

If you don't see these qualities in yourself, look for someone else that your child may be imitating. If your child is clearly imitating another guardian, relative, or friend, address that situation directly. Pay attention to your child's screen time. What are they playing on the computer or gaming system? What are they watching on tv? This influences their behavior. I remember so well, a phrase from a youth camp I attended long ago: "Garbage in, garbage out." We create our own lives, and part of how we do that is through outside influence. Outside influence creates thought patterns. Thought patterns create actions, etc. You see the connection.

Set your standards high for how you and your child will treat people. Be consistent with both expectations and discipline when your child treats people disrespectfully.

The bullying definition we use in this book (pages 17 and 90) can help you to evaluate your child's behavior, and the questions above can be answered by your child as well as yourself. Some children are more naturally empathetic to others and can clearly understand what hurts and what doesn't. Other children must be more clearly taught how their behavior affects others.

If your child manages Attention Deficit Hyperactivity Disorder (ADHD/ADD) or Fetal Alcohol Effect (FAE) or another barrier, they may need direct teaching about how their behavior affects others and supervision to understand consequences. They also require consistency in expectations—as do all children.

When Your Child is Using Victim Responses

When your child is using victim responses, you are likely to see fear of other students, low self-confidence, and a great deal of negative self-talk. You may see your child believing what another child is saying or withdrawing from peers. Your child may have a heightened fight or flight response, and be in a cycle of detrimental habits, including poor nutrition and lack of exercise/physical strength. There may be heightened negative perceptions of their physical self.

Bullying is not a one-time event for most children. They will usually experience various bullying behaviors throughout their young lives. Since their self-confidence and communication skills are critical to overcoming bully actions, the strategies offered here are intended as long-term solutions to help youth grow in these areas. Children who can communicate well and understand themselves and others are less likely to be bullied. They are more likely to judge and describe events as they are happening. They are also less likely to engage in bullying behavior themselves.

Parents and teachers alike find it difficult to decide whether to intervene in bullying situations. Though parents will express dismay over the treatment of their children, they aren't sure what to do. Children will sometimes express these struggles to their parents, and still ask their parents not to become involved, thus leaving parents helpless and confused. When your child does not want you to become actively involved in the situation, it becomes necessary to find behind-the-scene ways to help. This material helps you with that, allowing you to coach your child from the sidelines and help your child grow.

When Your Child is a Bystander

This is the opportunity every parent has, to give their child information. Even if you can't identify that your child is using bully actions, and even if your child has never made a disclosure that they are being bullied, you can approach them as if they are a bystander. The majority of children are, or will be, bystanders at some point in time.

The bystander role is the most important in the bullying cycle. While it might seem almost irrelevant, it has been shown to be the most effective strategy to change the culture of bullying. This only makes sense. Schools that are at risk need change. They need peaceful revolution that involves understanding each other, developing empathy and the decomposition of existing unhealthy cliques. This is where bystanders come in. Someone using bully actions isn't going to start the peaceful revolution. Someone experiencing bully actions isn't likely to be able to start the peaceful revolution. That is the role of the bystander.

Bystanders need all the same skills that children using bully actions and victim responses need. They need to be able to balance and understand their own thinking, and the thinking of others, develop empathy, and become strong communicators.

Self Esteem

There is a lot of talk about whether children who are frequently using bully actions have low self-esteem or high self-esteem.

I believe that either one of these may be the case.

A child that frequently uses bully actions may be living in a lifestyle of bullying. He may be bullied, leading to low self-esteem, building self-esteem through anger and aggressive action, and retaliation. A child may also have extremely high self-esteem, seeing other people as present to serve his ultimate purpose. He may view others with contempt; he may come from a family who is contemptuous of others.

Either way, a child frequently using bully actions needs to learn to understand others, understand themselves, feel and show empathy, communicate well, and understand the consequences to others of using those actions.

Role models need to examine the messages they are sending, even if it seems like the messages are being sent in a small way.

Teaching Points for Your Child

1. True bullying feeds on the fear of others. Teach your child how to minimize their fight or flight response in order to appear calm to one who is using bully actions. This is taught through breathing and relaxation exercises. When you are aware of how to relax yourself, you are then able to manage every situation that presents itself in a more positive fashion.

2. Bullying behavior by other children is a chance for your child to grow. Rather than acting simply in a protective role, teach your child how to manage the situation for themselves. Bullying behavior exists in both schools and workplaces. The time to bully-proof your child from workplace bullying actions is now.

3. Bullying behavior is unacceptable coming from YOU and your child. Point out behavior that you see as being inappropriate or hurtful to others. Allow your child to see you acting in positive ways toward others, and when you do hurt someone, allow them to know or see that you apologize, and that you work to heal with those that you have harmed.

4. Your child will increase in self-confidence by practicing and managing bullying behavior. Role-playing can help your child try out potential approaches. Have your child act the part of the child using a bully action while you respond. Then you act the part of the child using the bully action, allowing your child a chance to respond. Involve another person and take turns playing the bystander.

5. Work with your child to increase self-confidence and self-esteem in general. This happens actively as well as through role-modeling. Don't speak negatively about yourself. If you use terms such as "I'm a loser" when you make a mistake, your child learns HE is a loser when he makes a mistake. When you or your child make a mistake, turn it around and seek the learning experience from it. Teach your child that the purpose of mistakes and failures is to do better the next time. Teach your child to notice, identify and value his own positive qualities as well as those of others.

6. Give your child affirming messages. If you say to your child, "You are a pushover," your child begins to define themselves in that way. Turn it around and say instead, "I know you'll be able to stand up for yourself." Speak out loud the positives you see in your child. This will help your children define themselves in these positive ways, giving them strength to manage whatever situations may arise.

7. Teach your child that facing their fears increases confidence. Again, check your own role-modeling. Do you avoid problems?

8. Avoid the temptation of telling your child to return the bullying with physical violence. For most children this advice is unhelpful and simply reinforces a belief that personal power comes from violence-related strength.

9. Teach your child to use humor as a tool. A snappy comeback can diffuse conflict situations and create a more positive method of personal power. This only works if it is suited to your child's personality.

10. People with a High Bully Value Frame of Reference seek children they can scare. Teach your children to respond in ways that discourage further bullying action against them.

11. Teach your children to recognize inaccurate thinking. Explain to them that we all have thoughts about ourselves, others and the world that aren't quite right, and that we must challenge those thoughts.

Role-Playing

Role-playing is one of the most effective tools for teaching children how to manage bully actions and victim responses. This type of change management allows a child to control the situation and to learn, through practice, the exact thing they need. Role-playing may be used in schools and in families. It is an effective tool to teach skills that overcome both bully actions and victim responses.

Role-playing allows us to examine roles we're not used to and practice responses that we'll use later. Thinking ahead, outside our comfort zone, allows us to experiment, or improvise, rather than simply react to situations.

Although there are several techniques you can use to facilitate role-playing, some of the best involve improvisation, in which you don't use a formal script.

Discuss your child's situation with them to determine your child's needs. This also provides opportunity for the development of a closer relationship and better understanding of your child's day to day experiences.

Here is one example of a role-playing exercise to use with your child:

Child	(hits parent) Gimme your lunch!
Parent	(stepping back) Forget it!
	Other options: • Move to a location where adults are watching (review such locations with the child) • Respond with assertive phrases • Respond with humor • Team up with peers • Respond with extra kindness • Respond with silence, a steely glare and a relaxed body

Defining the Problem

It is important to pick your battles wisely. Defining a problem correctly will help you to decide the approach that needs to be taken. It will also help you to get people who seem to be on an 'opposite side', to help.

How the problem is defined makes a huge difference in how the conflict is approached, and ultimately resolved. If I come to you and tell you there is an issue with how you do things, and that it is affecting me in a negative way, you may not be interested in hearing about it. This way of speaking implies that the whole situation is a problem with how you are doing things. Typically, we have learned to define a problem in a way that is blaming. Our definitions of the issues are often unfair and biased toward being the fault of the person with whom we are in conflict.

Dr. Dan Dana says that the definition of a problem needs to be unbiased, objective, specific, resolvable and concise. Let's walk through those criteria, describe them, and look at the reasons they are important parts of a good definition.

- **Unbiased:** "free from bias; especially: free from all prejudice and favoritism: eminently fair." In order for a definition to be unbiased, it must not appear to favor either party.

- **Objective:** "expressing or dealing with facts or conditions as perceived without distortion by personal feelings, prejudices, or interpretations." An objective definition of a problem uses language and descriptions that are not blaming or criticizing.

- **Specific:** "free from ambiguity, accurate." A specific definition uses no assumptions. It is factual and specific about the problem needing to be resolved.

- **Resolvable:** "capable of being settled or resolved." The problem, as stated, must be resolvable. If the problem is that a school doesn't have enough equipment, and the meeting is between two teachers, defining the problem as "We need more equipment" makes it irresolvable. The two parties are unlikely to have the authority to purchase more equipment. If the definition is "We need to be able to work together better, using the limited equipment that we possess," then it is resolvable by the people who are meeting. The scope of the problem needs to be given limits to ensure that those involved in the meeting have the necessary authority to solve the problem.

- **Concise:** "marked by brevity of expression or statement: free from all elaboration and superfluous detail." The problem needs to be described in as few words as possible. An accurate definition is necessary, but the major focus needs to be toward resolution, rather than the history of the problem.

Defining the problem well puts the situation in perspective so that you can decide how, or if, you will work toward resolution.

Brainstorming

Brainstorming is the process of generating as many ideas as possible in a given (usually short and fixed) time. If some of the following are true it may be ineffective:

- the solution to your problem is clear,
- everybody agrees on what to do,
- either it's a simple problem, or only someone else can fix things, or both,
- nobody really can solve the problem at all.

With difficult problems, there is a temptation to take a limited view of possible solution methods, or even to throw up your hands and give up. If this is likely, of course brainstorming will not help at all.

In difficult situations, establish a list of needs prior to brainstorming. The list of needs can begin the idea creation. When the brainstorming exercise is complete, it can become a measuring stick to indicate if ideas will work or not, simply by asking the question, does this idea meet the needs?

Establish ground rules before you start:

- The group has one leader.
- The leader's only purpose is to keep things moving.
- The problem to be addressed is clearly understood by the entire group.
- Everyone has a chance to contribute. You can go around the table to solicit ideas, but this can pressure those who don't feel comfortable speaking up; on the other hand, if ideas are taken freestyle, vocal members of the group can dominate.
- Every contribution should be in that person's own words.

- No idea is criticized.

- The group has one recorder. You can have the recorder write everything on a board or flipchart, which would be easy for all to read; on the other hand, collecting Post-It Notes from each member of the group is easier on the recorder. Either way, it's important for the ideas to be in one place, where they can lead to more ideas.

Understanding and using the brainstorming process allows children to have a tool they can use to gather and evaluate ideas during difficult periods of time in their lives. Before brainstorming with your child for solutions to bullying, some needs to consider are:

- the need for safety,

- the need to change the situation,

- the need, as a bystander, to provide protection to someone else,

- the need for prevention of further bullying.

There is a strong temptation to criticize "bad ideas." This must be avoided, as it causes people to be afraid to give ideas.

After the brainstorming period is over:

- eliminate irrelevant ideas,

- group similar or related ideas,

- modify incomplete ideas,

- rank whatever ideas remain,

- discuss the ideas to see if they match the needs listed.

Pledging

Working with your child to prevent bullying issues is ongoing. Consider taking a pledge with your child, to show the commitment you have to each other and to learning through difficulties during these school years. Stay in touch with **No Such Thing as a Bully** through social media for easy access to tools discussed in the material. To get even more involved, and receive ongoing help in implementing all of these ideas, purchase a **No Such Thing as a Bully** Membership!

Goals

We're going to take a moment to work together to set your goals. Imagine being asked these questions and answer them for yourself as honestly as possible:

- What are the troublesome behaviors you see your child using?
- Who are the influential people in your child's life?
- How do they influence your child's behavior?
- How do you influence your child's behavior?
- What outcome would you like to see from using these protection lessons?

Self-Assessment of Your Own Communication Style

Consider the following questions. Also consider if you act in different ways with different people.

1. When a person finishes a conversation with me, does it seem like they feel respected? Do I feel good?

    If so, you are likely communicating assertively. You are treating others and yourself with respect. This type of behavior creates strong relationships and puts children in a good position to be positive bystanders.

2. Am I forceful with other people? Do I yell? Glare? Use other angry body language? Do I intimidate other people?

    If so, you are likely communicating aggressively. This type of behavior models and encourages bullying behavior in children.

3. Do I feel like I have been respectful to myself and my own needs? Am I doing things I don't want to do or am not comfortable with? Am I afraid, or do I find it awkward to say no?

    If so, you are likely communicating passively. This type of behavior can teach children to follow other children even if they are not comfortable with what is happening.

4. Do I do things for others and take care of them, without taking care of myself? Am I more worried about everyone else being okay than I am about myself being okay? Do I occasionally explode in anger? Do I refrain from telling a person exactly what I think, but talk about it with others afterwards?

    If so, you are likely communicating passive-aggressively. This type of behavior doesn't teach children to set boundaries or control their temper. They may be susceptible to bullying or conflicts with friends, or to becoming extremely stressed themselves.

Below are the four basic communication styles. Remember that you may use different types of behavior in different situations and with different people:

- **Assertive:** When you are assertive, you are respectful to yourself and to others. You meet your own needs while still being aware of the needs and feelings of others. You know that there are human rights and responsibilities that you must live by, such as the right to say no and the responsibility to do so clearly. You are aware that others have the same rights and responsibilities. You can speak out in order to meet your needs and you can do so in a way that is respectful of other people. You deal with conflict in a way that is respectful to all involved. You try to understand where others are coming from and work toward resolution that is fair to all the players involved.

- **Passive:** When you are passive, you are more respectful of other people than of yourself. You do not act directly to meet your own needs. You feel uncomfortable about coming right out and saying no. You feel that others take advantage of you, and you have trouble standing up for yourself. You go with the flow, even if you are unhappy about where the flow is taking you. You are sometimes described as a "doormat," because people "walk all over you." You will often choose to walk away from a conflict. You tend to withdraw, may have difficulty saying no and may have trouble making eye contact. You act in ways that smooth the waters. Your preference is to keep things calm rather than to meet your own needs. The result can be bitterness, unhappiness and a sense of others' taking advantage of your kindness.

- **Aggressive:** When you are aggressive you are more respectful to yourself than to other people. Using your aggressive behavior, you try to meet your own needs, but you do so at the expense of others. Others are harmed, either emotionally or physically by you. You will meet a conflict head on, using emotional, verbal or physical force to get your needs met. You don't worry about the needs of others. Sometimes you yell, threaten, and use frightening body language.

- **Passive-aggressive:** When you are passive-aggressive, you are not being respectful to anyone. You might be mostly passive, leading to a buildup of resentments until you become aggressive and blow up. You are unwilling to approach people with whom you are angry, but you talk behind their backs. You might even start rumors or seek ways to "get even." You are taking out aggression, but at a distance from the perceived offenders.

It is important to be aware of your communication and thought patterns, and the ways in which those have been passed on to your children. Keep in mind that this is about assessing, not judging. It is easier for children to become more assertive if their parents demonstrate assertive behavior. No parents—even the really, really good ones—are perfect. This isn't about measuring how bad you've been, it's about looking at places where you would like to be better.

PART 2

Protection Lessons for Parents and Children

Protection One: Conflict vs. Bullying

GOAL: To begin to understand and evaluate the differences between everyday conflict and bullying.

It is important for you to accept your child's perception of a situation and to try to understand the situation and its importance to your child. At times, the conflicts that children experience can seem small and are easily dismissed by busy parents. It may only be after repeated reporting that an adult identifies the situation as bullying.

You must listen to what your child is saying and monitor their experiences. You can start coaching your child very early by consistently addressing bully actions, such as hitting or taking others' belongings. You can model and practice appropriate reactions with your child when they are on the receiving end of bully actions. Explain to your child the importance of telling you when they, or others are being bullied. Telling can prevent serious trouble; it can keep someone from being hurt.

Keep in mind that these small conflicts are training ground for children to learn the communication and problem-solving skills that they will need as they grow. It is important not to take over their small conflicts. Instead, you must let them learn from these conflicts. But you must also keep them safe, so it is important to stay aware.

Activities:

1. Brainstorm examples of bully actions with your child. This is also nicely done with a group of siblings.

2. Brainstorm examples of disagreements with friends. Discuss whether or not these are bully actions. Why? Why not? Ask if there are power imbalances between the friends.

   If they get stuck, help them along with questions. Don't come up with their answers for them. Do ask questions that are relevant to their lives. Ask about interactions with specific friends, and/or at specific places.

Examples to assist with the brainstorming exercise include:

- Do you see any fighting at school? Are you involved in any fighting at school?
- Do you ever argue with your friends?
- When do you feel angry?

3. Create a story with your child. Writing it down creates a memory and an extra imprint of the information for both of you. It solidifies the issues you are working to manage.

Use the following guidelines.

- Make sure the story contains some of the discussion from the brainstorming session.
- Add a few sentences, then have your child add a few sentences.
- Do this activity slowly and add illustrations as you and your child wish.

4. Practice role-playing with your child. Switch roles, with each of you playing the child using the bully action, the child using the victim response, and as a bystander.

Use the examples you have created, or use the following examples:

- Some children are playing a rowdy sports game. One boy is continuously way too rough.
- Two children are talking. One wants to go to a movie, the other wants to go to a baseball game. One child pushes the other.
- Tommy has borrowed his friend Tina's music player. He has broken the player. Tina is yelling at Tommy.

5. Use the definition of bullying to evaluate the situations and see if bully actions are being used. If you need more information about the bullying definition first, skip ahead and read Protection Lesson 10.

6. Have your child create a story about bullying or an argument happening to an imaginary child. If this will be a chore, omit it. It is important that your child not feel this is extra homework!

7. If you or your child enjoys artwork, draw with them as you have this conversation. Or if your child is smaller and you like to draw, draw simple pictures that reflect the conversation and have your child color them in.

8. Invite your child to start a private journal. Tell them they are always welcome to share it with you, but the main part of having a journal is to learn to use it to figure out their thought patterns and their problems, and to also write about good things. Again, if your child finds this a chore, omit it, but a pleasant shopping trip for a nice book and fun pen for journaling can improve the chances of your child learning to use this valuable tool!

Protection Two: Feelings

GOAL: To be able to identify and express feelings.

As adults, we have learned to deny many feelings. We have learned to hide them—or they have morphed into something else, most likely anger. As a part of facilitating this process for your child, you are going to have to be in touch with your own feelings.

Anger is a secondary emotion. We express anger in conjunction with other emotions that society has labeled as "weaker" emotions—humiliation, confusion, frustration, sadness, distress, betrayal, helplessness, fear. These are the emotions that adults often refuse to let themselves express, even to themselves.

The refusal to express these emotions is something that is learned. You might have had parents who wanted you to toughen up. You might have had experiences that caused you to create a shell. You might have such strong feelings that even the thought of trying to figure them out is distressing. You might even think about closing this book right now. Please don't.

In order to resolve anger, emotions underneath anger must be addressed. You don't have to entirely figure out your own emotions in order to help your child, but it will help everyone with the journey.

Even if you don't understand your child's feelings, you can accept them. If you don't accept them, your child will stop telling you about them, possibly learning to bottle emotions, resulting in anger. Anger blocks positive relationships and creates inaccurate thinking.

Figuring out how you are feeling is difficult, both for adults and children. Find lists of feelings words online to help you along. Connect with **No Such Thing as a Bully** through social media for easy access to these extra tools. Don't let this difficulty block you or your child from pursuing this important basic ability.

All humans have a basic fight, flight, or freeze response when feeling threatened. A sense of threat can come from any negative emotion. When your body goes into fight or flight response, there is an increase in the amount of adrenaline that is pumped through your body. This causes a variety of changes! Your heart rate increases, the oxygen to your brain decreases (some people even see red), and your decision making is impaired. More blood and oxygen are transported to the large muscles, which will be used to fight or run. All those silly exercises, count to ten, take deep breaths, walk around the block... those are intended to get the oxygen back in your brain before you say (or do) something you regret.

Expect to be uncomfortable with some of your child's feelings. Again, acceptance is important. If some of the emotions that come up are about you, take a moment to examine your fight, flight, or freeze response, and refrain from becoming defensive. This is very important.

People can feel many emotions at the same time, including ones that would seem very contradictory.

When a child is in tune with his own feelings, he is more likely to be aware of the feelings of other people. Children need to understand that all human beings have the same kinds of emotions. Growth of empathy starts when you start teaching your child to understand his own feelings and the feelings of others.

Activities:

1. In order to lessen the pressure of you and your child opening up with your feelings, use other scenarios like the following to identify how other people are feeling.

   - Jill's parents are getting divorced. She is also having trouble with a boy at school who keeps on pestering her. Sometimes he pinches and hits her too. She doesn't know what to do. How do you think Jill is feeling?

   - Tom and James have been friends since kindergarten. They have argued and are angry with one another. They have said they won't be hanging out anymore. How do you think Tom and James are feeling?

   - Sally is on her way to a friend's party. Her parents were arguing last night. She had a pretty good day in school but didn't do as well on a test as she had hoped. How is Sally feeling?

   - You get caught up with a group of friends who are making fun of someone else. How is the person who is being made fun of feeling? How do you feel?

2. Read any book or passage that names several emotions. Talk with your child about the feelings mentioned in the book.

3. Search online for a list of feeling words. Using the list, make slips of paper with the words printed on them. Group the words into emotions that are similar. Group the words into emotions that you might feel at the same time. Use the words to play "emotions" charades. Use the list as you discuss the scenarios above as well.

4. Use magnetic letters to post today's expressed feelings on the refrigerator. Large families may wish to color code for each child. This is a great activity for adults to join in as well. Children need to learn that EVERYONE has feelings!

   Alternatively, help your children draw expressive faces for the family to choose from to post on the fridge or a bulletin board, or search emotion faces online.

Protection Three: Fight, Flight, or Freeze

GOAL: To understand and manage our personal biological response to threatening situations and thoughts.

This lesson explores the fight, flight or freeze response further. Please note that in referring to fight, flight or freeze, response and reaction are used interchangeably.

The symptoms of a fight, flight, or freeze response are as follows:

- increased heart rate
- increase in adrenaline
- upset or butterfly stomach
- tense muscles
- fast, sometimes regrettable verbal or physical reactions
- quick thoughts/seeing red

For some people, the response includes freezing of thought and/or physical abilities.

Think about times when you have experienced a fight, flight, or freeze reaction. What are the things that sent you into that mode? What are the situations or phrases that you find threatening? Often a threat to your parental authority (such as a child talking back) will cause a fight, flight, or freeze reaction.

Again, in combination with the fight, flight, or freeze reaction, remember that anger has an underlying emotion. To dissolve a reaction, the underlying emotion and threat must be recognized. Once it is, it can be addressed and removed. Remaining adrenaline can be removed through physical activity and relaxation practice.

Dissolving this reaction is essential to becoming more assertive. Becoming more assertive helps you and your child manage others' bad behavior in a calm and capable way.

Activities:

1. Explain to your child the relationship between adrenaline and the fight, flight, or freeze reaction.

2. Brainstorm how you and your child are affected by fight, flight, or freeze reactions. Discuss what kinds of things bring on fight, flight, or freeze reactions for each of you and how that reaction feels. (To keep it child-appropriate, avoid discussing work conflict or conflict with your spouse).

3. Take your pulse; teach your child how and help them to do the same. Run in place for a minute. Each of you take your pulse again. Talk about how an elevated heart rate feels. Talk about the difference between elevating your heart through exercise versus the fight, flight, or freeze reaction. What are the differences in how your body feels?

4. Brainstorm and practice activities your child likes that use up extra adrenaline.

5. Lie down and practice breathing deeply together. Try to time your breathing to your child's breathing to make it comfortable for your child. Put your hand on your stomach, and on your child's stomach to show how, when you breathe in, your stomach expands. Depending on the age of your child and the relationship you have with them, you may wish to have them lay their head on your stomach and feel the motion that happens when you breathe deeply.

6. Explore age-appropriate meditations with your child. Many can be easily found online.

7. Connect online with **No Such Thing as a Bully** and ask for the two-minute relaxation exercise. Follow the instructions and practice the exercise together.

8. Role-play threatening situations. These may be bullying situations or dinosaur attacks or any other situation that your child is interested in. Mirror some of the stories discussed in previous protection lessons, particularly for older children. After the role play, ask them to describe how they feel. Is their heart going faster? Are they sweating?

9. Notice your own fight, flight and freeze reactions and those of your child in the weeks and months to come. Actively work to practice getting the response under control.

Protection Four: Important Ideas

GOAL: To understand some basic principles of communication that tend to build positive relationships.

Idea One

Good communication skills help you to stand up for yourself. They also help you to avoid and resolve conflict.
If you and your child can communicate well, you will have less conflict throughout your lives. When conflict arises, you will be better equipped to handle it. When people use bully actions, you will have more tools to be able to deflect them.

Idea Two

Conflict and bullying are two different things. Conflict is found in many everyday situations and can help your child to learn. Being able to distinguish between conflict and bullying is important.

Idea Three

Everyone is going to have a different perception. Every story has several sides to it. Trying to understand perceptions can help to increase empathy in children.
Remember that your child, regardless of age, is not going to have the same perceptions as you, even while experiencing a common situation.

Idea Four

The fight, flight, or freeze reaction is natural, but you can learn more balanced ways of approaching threats.
You can keep your own reaction and other people's reactions in mind when you are dealing with conflict, or even with bullying. You can use relaxation techniques and balanced thinking strategies to control your own reactions. You can learn to moderate your approach so that you can help other people keep their reactions down too.

Idea Five

Most people do not want to escalate problems, but they do not have an understanding of positive approaches or conflict minimization strategies.

When you are trying to deal with a bullying situation, keep in mind that you might be better able to communicate about the problem than the other person. The other parents, teachers, principals, school boards may all experience a fight, flight, or freeze reaction in hearing about your child's issue. Remember to help out the other person by staying calm and providing some ideas for solutions.

Idea Six

Be aware of your personal reactions. You must be aware of what causes you to react. For some people it is being called a certain name. For others it is seeing someone else being hurt. During certain times in your life you are under more stress than others, which affects your personal reactions. Know and examine your reactions in order to learn more about yourself.

Idea Seven

If you understand that people have different perceptions, open discussion will result in genuine and often unique solutions.

Even when bullying is severe and when it is based in contempt, open discussion is necessary. There needs to be an understanding of what happened from each person's point of view. A person who is contemptuous learns to be empathetic by understanding the emotions and situations of others. Speaking openly about conflict can help you understand the perception of the other person. Be open to receiving this information, rather than feeling threatened because your perceptions differ. This shift in understanding moves the conflict forward and opens up the discussion so you can brainstorm solutions that will best meet the needs of everyone.

Explain the ideas to your child at their level. The following alternate explanations may help:

We both need to make sure we have the words and ideas to respond to bullying. Being assertive will keep us from using bully actions or victim responses.

Bullying and conflict are two different things. It is important to know the difference between the two.

People must understand each other's perceptions and how they see the world.

We have a fight, flight, or freeze response when we feel threatened. So does the other guy! We need to help him stay calm.

Having ideas and words to stand up to bullying peacefully is important. We need to share our ideas.

It is important to know about ourselves, to know when we feel angry and when we feel sad. If we know how we feel, it's easier to tell others what we need.

Talking about problems will help you to solve them. It helps you understand the other person and get rid of assumptions. Listen to understand.

Activities:

1. Discuss the fight, flight, or freeze reaction again, talking about the lesson you used previously.

2. Discuss assumptions. Discuss the question, "Do you know this for sure?" This is best done through natural conversation. Talk about times that you made assumptions and were wrong. Help your child find times that he did the same.

3. Talk about listening. Be completely silent for a short period of time. Then talk about what you hear when you are listening, instead of making noise.

4. Talk openly about your child's perception of differences in the lifestyles they see around them. They may know children with one or two parents; they may know children from different cultures. Discuss differences, placing value on everyone.

5. Practice finding out about "someone" with your child through role play. Ask your child to make up a character.

She doesn't have to have all the details in mind. Now, you ask open questions of your child as that person. Find out as much as you can about the pretend person. Switch roles after 10 minutes or when you run out of questions and answers. Reverse roles. Protection Lesson 14 contains information about types of questions and may be reviewed before this activity.

6. Have your child practice finding out about and understanding real people—other family members and friends. This almost becomes an interview process, and your child discovers how to learn about someone—a very important friendship skill.

Protection Five: The Bullying Spiral

GOAL: To understand how bullying develops and the points in time when it can be stopped.

APPROACH and GROOMING: One person is approached by another. If the approaching person has learned to control by power, the grooming pattern includes testing to see how this person will react.

> STOPPER: You need to be able to set boundaries right here. If the approaching person sees that he cannot control the other, the testing is not successful. Being able to stand up for yourself and others, starts here. A lot of bully actions can be prevented when you are able to do this.

DELIBERATE THREATS OR TEASING and REPEATED HARMFUL ACTIONS: If the approaching person feels he CAN have some power over the other person, the teasing, threats and/or harmful actions continue. They will accelerate as long as the situation is not addressed, and the victim responses continue.

> STOPPER: Your child must know that you are prepared to listen and help if he tells you he is repeatedly experiencing bully actions at the hands of his peers. Encourage your child to TELL if he or someone else is being repeatedly bullied.

PEER INFLUENCE/OTHERS' PERCEPTIONS: Peer influences play a very big part in the bullying spiral and can directly affect whether bullying will continue or not. If bullying is cheered on by peers—or even just ignored—it is likely to continue. It has been shown that a child will eventually reconsider using bully actions if the desired reaction of receiving peer support is not achieved.

> STOPPER: Your child needs to understand how very important it is for them to step up for another child when they see bully actions happening. They need to understand how to become friends with others, so that they—and others—have a positive support group.

STEREOTYPING: Players in the scenario may be characterized as bully and victim. If this happens for your child, their self-concept may begin to develop around that negative label.

> STOPPER: Reassure your child that bully actions and victim responses are simply behaviors that get used. Every person has the power to use different behaviors. Work together to practice eliminating bully actions and victim responses by using assertive behaviors.

HURT BEFORE BEING HURT: The child using victim responses is likely to feel helpless and may lash out at others. As they define themselves as a victim, their behavior becomes a habit. The child using bully actions may feel helpless to change their behavior. They will make a lot of sacrifices in terms of peer group status if they change their behavior. As they define themselves as a bully, their behavior becomes a habit.

> STOPPER: Pay attention to your child's behaviors, and work with them to replace bully actions and victim responses with assertive behavior; to develop empathy if needed; to strengthen a positive self-concept; and to enhance friendship skills. Address issues with peers and provide opportunities for introduction to new peer groups.

At the height of the spiral, destruction or mutual self-destruction may result. This can even be an automatic stress response, such as a person who is bullied snapping and physically hurting someone. This may have happened in the case of Richard Gale and Casey Heynes (Shippey). Another scenario includes children, who feel they have been victimized, making plans for revenge on a grand scale, such as in Columbine. Suicide is another method of destruction which impacts those who have used bully actions. In some situations, people have been charged and convicted for bully actions leading to someone's suicide. There is no good stopper here. We must stop the spiral before this point.

Activities:

1. Use the explanation above to explain the Bullying Spiral to your child.

2. Brainstorm and discuss real life bullying situations that escalated. Do some internet research. Describe how they might have gone through these processes.

3. Role-play a bullying situation with three or more people. Have one or more people stand up for the person who is being bullied. Talk about how that affects the situation.

4. Role-play a bullying situation where your child is alone. Have your child practice standing up for himself. Reverse the roles and keep practicing.

Protection Six: Working Through Harm

Knowing how and when to say you are sorry, and MEANING it is tremendously important. There are essentially two ways to come to repentance—self-centered repentance and other-centered repentance.

A person can get caught and feel sorry they've been caught. This repentance is self-centered and tends to be less effective in the long term. It is not based on understanding.

It is important to move from self-centered repentance to other-centered repentance. This happens when you accept your own behavior and begin to understand the other person. You come to see the reason why your behavior is hurtful.

With other-centered repentance, you feel sorry that you have been involved in something that has hurt someone else. You are quickly able to identify when you need to apologize and mean it. You are more likely to be able to work through "the three R's" of restitution, resolution and reconciliation, as outlined in Barbara Coloroso's work in *The Bully, The Bullied, and The Bystander*.

1. **Restitution**: This means fixing the problem that has been created. If an item has been damaged, it must be replaced, if damaging rumors have been spread, the offender must step up and admit to spreading untrue rumors. Physical harm is more difficult to fix, and the regaining of trust is a process that takes time and is earned by changed behavior. In this material, it will be referred to simply as fixing the problem.

2. **Resolution**: This means preventing another incident from happening. There are three steps to this: accepting what happened, understanding why it happened—and your own emotions around it—and learning something positive from it. In this material, it will be referred to simply as prevention—preventing another incident from happening.

3. **Reconciliation**: This is the process of healing alongside the person you have hurt. Because safety of the person harmed is so important, they cannot be forced to be involved in a reconciliation process. A reconciliation process for the other child is still possible. A great question

to ask is "What can I do to help the person I have hurt have a better time?" or "What can I do to help other people in general?" Coloroso identifies that this helps a child to "be good and do good", providing an opportunity that is the antithesis to bullying.

When your child is involved in bullying, whether as the primary child or as one who has been co-opted to support the bullying, you must help them to understand how their action has affected the other person. Whether or not they acknowledge the hurt they have caused, they must still work through the consequential three R's.

Repentance will often lead to an apology, but without sincerity and a change in behavior, apologies are not terribly helpful. Restitution, resolution and reconciliation may lead to sincere repentance.

When your child has used a bully action, working through this process allows him to understand that he is just a person who did something wrong. Simply put, it is not WHO he is, rather, it is what he has done and these are steps he can take to repair the wrong he has done.

Something to note is that when you are in a situation where you are working well with the other person, and you are creating the opportunity to be involved in good works, a Serotonin Response is created. Basically, instead of producing a lot of fight, flight, or freeze adrenaline, the body is increasing its production of serotonin—the feel-good hormone that keeps us from falling into a depression.

Bringing this down to a level for younger children means that you must parent consistently using the three R's (restitution, resolution and reconciliation) with your children when you see bully actions. They must go through the following three steps, and work through them with your help.

1. How can you fix this?

2. How can you stop this from happening again?

3. What can you do that is being good and doing good and helping someone else?

Activities:

1. Use the explanation above to explain the steps to your child. Ask your child if there was a time when they did something wrong and felt sorry right away. What happened? Did they apologize? Did they change their behavior? Tell your child about a time when you did.

2. Using the three Rs, work through the following scenarios that bring bully actions to their logical end point.

Samantha and Julie have been good friends. Recently Samantha has been hanging around with some other girls and sometimes she treats Julie meanly. Lately she has been verbally 'teasing' Julie about her clothes. and Samantha's friends have posted mean comments to Julie's Facebook page. Julie feels excluded and hurt.

Questions to ask:

- How responsible is Samantha for the situation? How responsible are her new friends?

- How can Samantha work through restitution? How can she fix this?

- How can Samantha work through resolution? How can she make sure she isn't involved in this kind of behavior again?

- How can Samantha work through reconciliation? What can she do to make things better for Julie?

John has been using bully actions for a long time and a lot of children are afraid of him. He has a big following, and seems popular, because no one wants to cross him and become one of his targets. Finally, a small group of children have decided to group together and tell an adult what is happening.

Questions to ask:

- How can adults help John work through the three R's?

- How responsible is John for the situation?

- How can he work through restitution? How can he fix this?

- How can John work through resolution? How can he make sure he stops using bully actions?

- How can John work through reconciliation? What can he do to make things better for kids at school, and for other people?

- How can John understand the point of view of the people affected by his bully actions?

- Do you think that John will feel sorry for his actions when he works through the three R's?

Mandy and Kyle are friends and they both like each other. Mandy gets invited to a party that Kyle is not invited to, and she really wants to go. She lies to Kyle about it and says she is doing something with her family. Kyle phones her that night and catches her in the lie.

This is a little more complicated! Some questions:

- Is this a bully action? Check the definition again and see if it fits. If it doesn't fit, can the three R's still be used?

- Why do you think Mandy lied? How do you think she might feel? How do you think Kyle might feel?

- How can Mandy work through restitution and fix this?

- How can Mandy work through resolution to make sure she stops using that type of behavior?

- How can Mandy work through reconciliation? Do you think Kyle will be willing to work through it with her? What can she do to make things better for Kyle?

To gain a fuller understanding and for ideas about how this could be applied to situations currently in the media, connect with **No Such Thing as a Bully** through social media and start a discussion!

Protection Seven: How You Act

GOAL: To learn the types of behavior and move toward assertion.

- **Aggressive:** You have respect for your own needs, but not for the needs of others. You are likely to be at risk of using bully actions. Examples: yelling, name-calling, hitting, threatening, belittling

- **Passive:** You respect the needs of others, but not your own. You may be at risk of being a 'doormat' and using victim responses. Examples: going along with the group, even if the group is going against what you want; saying yes when you would rather say no.

- **Passive-Aggressive:** You don't respect yourself, or others. You may use bully actions sometimes and victim responses other times. Examples: being nice to someone to their face, but mean behind their back; doing a lot for someone and then blowing up instead of just saying no.

- **Assertive:** You are respectful of yourself and others. You speak your mind clearly and respectfully. You are unlikely to use bully actions or victim responses. Examples: speaking up respectfully right away when someone treats you badly; saying no when you mean no and yes when you mean yes.

You've seen these behaviors before when you used the self-assessment tool to determine how you use the behaviors. Anyone can use any of the behaviors in different situations. You might be passive with your children, and aggressive with your sister, or passive with your boss and aggressive with your children. Your behavior might fluctuate depending on mood and life circumstances. Being able to evaluate and understand your own behavior gives you power. Helping your child gain this skill involves him as part of his own life plan and gives him power. Having a sense of involvement and power in your life is one of the biggest self-esteem builders available, and building a positive self-concept is an important part of bullyproofing a child.

Understanding that these are behaviors, not personalities, is important. If you see someone as aggressive, it will be hard to look at them in a positive manner. If you see someone as using aggressive behavior, your interactions are likely to end up being more positive.

Interestingly, it seems to be assertive behavior that increases a person's serotonin level the most, while the other behaviors increase adrenaline and encourage a fight, flight, or freeze response.

Activities:

1. Identify that passive is often the same as "flight or freeze" and aggressive is often the same as "fight" in the fight, flight, or freeze response. When we flee from threats or conflict, we may do so by physically running away, but we may also do it by being fearful of saying no and letting people take advantage of us. When we fight against threats or conflict, we often use aggressive words or behaviors to display our fight reaction. This increases our adrenaline!

2. Look for examples of these types of behavior going forward, and directly point them out to your child. Also point out when your child seems to feel happy and remind them of the serotonin response. Help your child to learn to notice and understand the connections between what they are doing and how they feel, particularly when the connections are positive. This helps develop your child's positive self-concept and confidence. (If the relationship with your child is strained, be careful with this. Using the exercise to primarily identify negative behaviors will backfire, as will using it insincerely.)

3. Use the five following scenarios to help your child understand each type of behavior. Understanding what kind of behavior someone is using helps your child decide how to react. It allows your child to choose their reactions instead of simply reacting.

    a. Jed can be very loud. He'll often keep persuading and persuading until people do what he wants. Sometimes he threatens them or gets mad and yells at them. People tend to try to avoid him although he has a group of friends that seem to stay with him just the same. What kind of behavior is Jed using? (aggressive)

b. Sandy thinks of himself as an easygoing kind of guy. He just kind of tags along with his friends and doesn't make too many demands about what he wants to do. One night, Sandy and his friends end up at a party. They decide to go throw eggs at someone's house. Sandy tags along but doesn't feel happy about what is happening. What kind of behavior is Sandy using? (passive)

c. Praema has been helping her friend Brenna with homework. Lately Brenna is just expecting Praema to do it. Praema doesn't know how to tell her she isn't going to do it for her, so she keeps on doing it. Finally, Praema gets so angry that she ends the relationship with Brenna, but never tells her what is wrong. What kind of behavior is Praema using? (passive-aggressive)

d. Marie and Nancy have had an argument. Marie is very popular and has been spreading rumors about Nancy. She has also told her friends not to talk to Nancy at all. What kind of behavior is Marie using? (passive-aggressive)

e. Jonathan's parents are worried about him. Since changing to a bigger school, he has more friends that live farther away than before. His parents don't know where his friends live or even who many of them are. They want to give him stricter rules, and not let him go anywhere after school. Jonathan suggests that he write all the names of his friends and their addresses down for his parents and agrees to leave notes about where he is going, and phone and leave a message if he is somewhere else. His parents suggest having a small party where they could meet his new friends and then leave to a different part of the house, and just check in occasionally. What kind of behavior are Jonathan and his parents using? (assertive)

6. Do impromptu role plays and help your child decide what kind of behavior was acted out. Here are some examples:

   a. Two children are playing a game. One child is losing and throws the game board to the ground, waves his fist in the other's face, and stomps off. (Aggressive)

   b. Jenna and Sara are walking down the street. Jenna wants to throw rocks at an old building. Sara says she doesn't want to, but Jenna doesn't listen. Sara ends up throwing the rocks too. (Passive)

   c. Josh and Marie used to like each other. Now Marie is mad at Josh. Instead of talking to him about the problem, she is spreading bad rumors about him at school. (Passive-Aggressive)

   d. Ben and Arnie agreed to hang out on Saturday, but now they want to do different things. Ben wants to play video games, and Arnie wants to go for a bike ride. Arnie also wants Ben to help him deliver his papers. They talk about it and agree that they will deliver the papers using bikes, go for a ride, come back and play video games. (Assertive)

Protection Eight: Friendship Skills

GOAL: To understand positive friendship qualities and evaluate relationships.

Sometimes we make a wonderful friendship connection and the relationship is easy to maintain. Essentially, we don't have to think very much about being that person's friend.

In life, though, situations arise where friendships can be more difficult. Children are thrown into situations where friendship skills are tremendously important. They may feel isolated and afraid, particularly when there are bully actions against them. They may feel they have no outlet for their feelings, or that when they do try to express what is happening, they are ignored and further isolated. Children who are experiencing bully actions can alleviate some of their problems by learning strong friendship skills.

Often professionals talk about befriending the person using bully actions. That can be a solution, but it can also create a situation where a child has acquired a "friend" they are afraid to cross. It puts them at risk of becoming a user of bully actions. When it works in a balanced way, it can be a good thing. Otherwise, your child needs to know how to make friends of OTHER children—friends he hasn't met yet that might be a support. Also, he needs to know how to keep the friends he has, during the bullying episode.

Friendships include different components at different stages:

- **Early childhood:** In early childhood, your child begins to understand the need for taking turns, but they tend to be egocentric, centered on themselves. Friendship is based on simple play, and friends are the ones who are in the same room with them.

- **Elementary age (Grades 1 to 4):** In elementary school, children begin to experience friendships that include give and take. Children begin to associate with others who they see as similar to them in some way, most often in likes and dislikes.

- **Middle school age (Grades 5 to 8):** In middle school, children are very aware of their effect on their peers and what is said about them. They are also more aware of what they say about others, and the effects it all has. Importance is placed on loyalty, and certain expectations of trust are in place. Friendships are based in common interests and developed through experience sharing. Cliques may form, as children become choosy about their friends. A split between genders is likely to be seen.

- **High School (Grades 8 to 12):** Peer group acceptance is of the ultimate importance. Family is often rejected in favor of peers. Loyalty and trust are expected in friendships. Friendships are formed with people who make your child feel understood, recognized and supported. There is increased understanding when different types of friendships can be experienced.

Friendship skills include:

- being able to introduce yourself to a group.
- starting and maintaining conversations.
- being able to ask questions to find out about others.
- awareness and control of tone of voice.
- listening and trying to understand.
- understanding and empathizing with mistakes.
- accepting people for who they are.
- giving and accepting compliments.
- giving and accepting criticism.
- giving and accepting help.
- being cooperative.
- being able to negotiate and problem solve.
- supporting a friend in difficult times.
- supporting a friend in positive growth.
- sharing your space, and your stuff.

- being a good winner and a good loser.
- knowing how to ignore annoyances.
- choosing friends.

When you see your child using these skills, give them positive feedback. Positive feedback encourages more positive behavior.

Activities:

1. Discuss with your child how they feel when they try to introduce themselves:
   - In a group where no one knows each other
   - In a group where people know each other, but do not know your child
   - In a group where they know the people a little bit but are not good friends

2. With your child, role-play jumping into a conversation and/or introducing yourselves. Practice welcoming another child into a conversation by turning your body toward them and widening the talking space circle.

3. If your child is experiencing bully actions, talk about the friends they have. Are they good friends? Are there opportunities to make new friends, or to expand on friendships that are already slightly developed?

4. Brainstorm ways to meet/introduce yourselves to new people. Use the introduction situations above to develop role plays.

5. To enhance listening skills, make a habit of reading with your child. Every two or three pages, ask your child to summarize what happened. If a book is complicated, ask for a summarization more often, or if your child is advanced, ask for a summarization at the end, and ask other questions about what happened. This gives your child experience in listening and rephrasing. Empathizing can

also be enhanced by discussing the feelings, or potential feelings of the characters, throughout reading.

6. Talk about compliments in the following way with your child, using the idea for yourself as well.

   A compliment is a gift that can be given for free. It is important to accept a compliment with a simple, "Thank you," rather than trying to deny it or immediately return another compliment.

7. Learning to accept people as they are can start by helping people. Seek out a soup kitchen or food bank, where you can help as a family. Help your child to see that we need to define people by their inner selves, not their outer trappings. Help them see that every person has an important place in the world.

8. Brainstorm some arguments that your child has had with friends and define the two positions (e.g., one person wants to go to the movie, one wants to go to the youth center) Work through the situation using a friendship problem solving process. Help your child to ask the following questions about the disagreement:

   - Why was my position important to me?
   - Why was the other person's position important to them?
   - Is there an obvious compromise? (Can we do both things?)
   - Is there a possible trade off? (We do what you want tonight, and what I want next time.)

9. Talk openly about jealousy. Are there ever times when you or your child feel jealous of the other person in a friendship? Jealousy tends to be related to one's own self-concept. Discussing jealousy can bring into focus the needs a child has, in terms of self-concept development. If your daughter is jealous of a friend because the friend is thinner, it points out a body self-concept issue that needs focus. REMEMBER, changing self-concept is not about finding and changing the perceived negatives. It is about finding and enhancing the real positives.

10. To practice ignoring annoyances, practice ignoring annoyances! When you, or your child are annoyed by someone's behavior, ask yourselves "How much will this matter in six months?" (or even tomorrow). For minor annoyances, the answer is not at all. This helps you and your child to think about it in a balanced way. When a behavior cannot be ignored, teach your child distraction. For example, when their sibling is tapping their pen against the table, a child can get up and go to a different room for a different activity without bothering to make a comment.

11. Have your child keep a friendship diary. They can keep track of each time they use a friendship skill.

12. Brainstorm a list of important qualities they want their friends to have and compare their good friends with the list. Do their good friends have those qualities? Brainstorm a list of qualities that would make them choose not to have someone for a friend.

Protection Nine: Bill of Rights and Responsibilities

GOAL: To learn and practice the Assertive Bill of Rights and Responsibilities.

The Bill of Rights and Responsibilities is the basis for assertive behavior. Learning and living the ideas in it will prevent both bully actions and victim responses. To print copies of the bill for your bulletin boards or refrigerator, connect with **No Such Thing as a Bully** on social media and ask for them!

Bill of Rights and Responsibilities

1. You have the right to be treated with respect. You have the responsibility to ask for respect, to respect others in return, and to respect yourself.

2. You have the right to have and express your own opinions and feelings. You have the responsibility to do that respectfully and to take responsibility for owning your feelings and opinions.

3. You have the right to be listened to and taken seriously. You have the responsibility to express yourself clearly, simply and calmly and to take yourself seriously on serious matters.

4. You have the right to set your own priorities. You have the responsibility to take the time and effort to follow through.

5. You have the right to say "No" without feeling guilty or making excuses. You have the responsibility to say "No" honestly and directly.

6. You have the right to ask for what you want knowing that others have the same right to say "No."

7. You have the right to ask for information from any source. You have the responsibility to decide if the information is helpful and whether to make use of it.

8. You have the right to make mistakes. You have the re-

sponsibility to accept that you don't have to be perfect and the responsibility to learn from your mistakes.

9. You have the right to change your mind. You have the responsibility to accept the consequence of doing so.

10. You have the right to not know all the answers. You have the responsibility to accept that you don't have to know everything and can research the answer, if you wish.

11. You have the right to tell someone you want to take time to think things over. You have the responsibility of doing so and getting back to the other party with your clear answer.

12. You have the right to choose not to assert yourself. You have the responsibility to accept the effects of not asserting yourself and feel okay about it.

Activities:

1. Be sure to have a discussion about times when your child is not allowed to say no, such as when facing a needle at the doctor's office or when there is homework to be done. It's important that children know that they can say no at times; and they also must know when they can't.

2. Depending on the age of your child, you may wish to discuss how not living according to the rights and responsibilities can result in criminal activity. For example, when you engage in stealing you are not respecting the rights of others. You are not respecting others' property. You are not respecting yourself and your positive abilities.

3. Especially for younger children, ask your child if there are any words in the rights and responsibilities that are difficult to understand.

4. Discuss some, or all, of the following questions with your child. Don't worry about having the 'right' answers. The importance of this exercise is in the discussion. Simply talk about different situations and ideas with your child.

    a. How do we know if we are respecting ourselves and

others? What kinds of behaviors do we see?

b. What kinds of ideas and emotions are hard to express?

c. What are some ways that we can express ourselves clearly?

d. When have you said no?

e. What kinds of things might others say no to you about?

f. When might you not want to answer yes or no right away?

g. What are some examples of times when you must get information from other people?

h. What are some examples of learning from mistakes?

i. What are some examples of times when you have changed your mind or when you might change your mind? What might be some of the consequences of changing your mind?

j. What kinds of things don't you know the answers to? Discuss the phrase, "You don't know what you don't know" (Anonymous).

k. When might you decide not to act assertively? (This can be a tough one, so some examples are: When you have to do something anyway, like homework; when it is best to walk away from a situation and think about what you are going to do about it.)

12. With your child, draw a picture of a time they made a mistake and discuss what was learned.

13. We can learn something extremely well by teaching. Encourage your child to teach the rights and responsibilities to another adult who is important in their lives.

Protection Ten: Bully Actions and Victim Responses

At this point, you've learned a lot about communicating and have a lot of things to teach your child. Now we're into the meat and potatoes of the issue.

By now, you also know that this is a whole new approach to the bullying issue. Whether your child is using bully actions, or victim responses, they are first and foremost A CHILD—YOUR CHILD. Not a victim, and not a bully, but rather, a child who is using bully actions, or a child who is using victim responses.

The definition of bullying that is used in this program is as follows:

High Bullying Value (HBV) Frame of Reference =	desire to hurt + superior power/ enjoyment + desire for control/ contempt
ACTION =	hurtful + repeated
High Victim Response (HVR) Frame of Reference =	vulnerability + sense of oppression/ unjust treatment

Bullying can thus be described in equation form (Rigby):

Bullying = HBV + ACTION + HVR

Here is a simpler view for younger children.

You are bullying if you:

1. want to hurt someone.

2. do something that hurts them.

3. are stronger than them in some way and use that extra power to hurt them.

4. hurt them intentionally more than once.

5. enjoy hurting people, and think you are better than they are.

6. the people you hurt feel sad, bad and helpless.

You are experiencing bullying if:

1. someone wants to hurt you

2. someone does something that hurts you.

3. the person is stronger than you in some way and uses that extra power to hurt you

4. the person hurts you more than once.

5. the person enjoys hurting you

6. you feel hurt, sad, bad and helpless.

It is important to understand the bully prevention strategies that are used in your child's school. Don't be afraid to get involved! A school's number one complaint about bully prevention programs is not having the manpower to implement and maintain a full program. Parents need to get involved in order to create a culture of involvement. Involvement is also a part of teaching your child to "do good, be good and will good" (Coloroso). Become involved in the school with a positive mind set and the intention to help create a safe happy setting for all children. This doesn't need to be about protecting your child or "keeping an eye on the bully."

Breaking the definition down into parts makes it easier to understand. Be sure your child understands the definition and understands how the definition is used to evaluate behavior and decide if it is bullying behavior.

Depending on the age of your child, you may also have to address sexual bullying and sexual assault. You also need to be aware of sexual identity bullying. Most often sexual identity bullying comes from home. Has your child ever heard you say "That's so gay," or "limp-wristed", or "fairy", or "butch"? Evaluate carefully, because a lot of people DO make comments like this from time to time. Children WILL notice and mirror this.

Remind yourself and your child that you may not even know who in their lives is LGBTQIA+. They may be making comments about a classmate's sexuality, and find out years later that their own brother is gay or their wife's sister is transgender.

Sexual identity is an easy bully action tool to use because people tend to feel uncomfortable addressing it. Identify it and don't make talking about it embarrassing. The less secretively sexual identity issues are treated, the less bully action power the issues have.

Make sure your child knows that there are many kinds of bullying and explain them all. The types of bullying include physical, verbal, emotional, sexual, sexual identity, and cyber bullying, through phone and internet.

Your child needs to be aware that they have a big negative effect on people when they use bully actions.

Discuss the following effects:

- fear of being in an area of the school where bully actions take place. (This might even be the bathroom; imagine being afraid to go to the bathroom!)

- lower grades, poor attendance, less concentration

- difficulty making or keeping friends, sometimes due to the pressure of the bully on other people as well.

Let your child know that students who are bullied are frightened and need friends. Help them understand that it is good to befriend someone who is bullied but also that he may need adult help with the situation.

Explain to them that when someone is using bully actions, it is because they are trying to feel strong and powerful. The person using bully actions can ONLY look strong and powerful if the person they are using bully actions against gets upset. They continue to use bully actions on those who look timid or frightened, those who give them an "entertaining" reaction. (Entertaining reactions tend to be based in the fight, flight, or freeze response.)

When you are using bullying actions, you need to:

1. Learn about feelings—especially anger and sadness. Feeling angry or sad can make you want to treat others badly.

2. Learn about positive ways to handle your feelings, and make sure that you have an adult that you can talk to about your feelings.

3. Learn how to talk in a respectful way.

4. Learn respectful ways to get what you want and need.

5. Tell your parents or another adult that you need some help if something has changed in your life and it is making you angry, sad or mad. This might be a new baby, someone dying, your parents divorcing, or anything else that bothers you.

Bullying actions can go on because, a person who is receiving bully actions might:

1. Be afraid to stand up to the person using them

2. Feel like they are all alone and have no one to go to for help.

3. Feel bad about themselves and feel like they deserve to be treated badly.

4. Feel that things will only get worse if they try to stop the bully actions.

5. Hope that if they do what the person wants, the person will start to be their friend.

When you are being bullied:

1. Tell someone! Your parents, your grandparents or your teacher, but make sure you tell someone! You can tell them who was involved and if anyone else saw it happen. You can tell them where it happened and how often it has happened. If you have any injuries, scrapes or bruises make sure you show them to an adult.

2. Be a friend to someone else who is being hurt. Most often people using bully actions don't want to pick on kids who are in groups.

3. Stay away from people who use bully actions if you can. Try ignoring them and walking away. They can't use the

bully action on you unless you are there. If it is happening online, go offline completely for several weeks.

4. Stay where teachers or adults can see you. If they can see you being hurt, they will be able to help you, especially if you have made them aware of the bully actions.

5. Don't bring expensive things or lots of money to school.

6. Be confident. People using bully actions like to pick on kids who seem scared. Hold your head up and stand up straight.

7. Don't fight back. Think up things to say ahead of time. Use "I" statements. (Protection Lesson 12) Don't say things that are mean. Deal with the bully action without using a bully action yourself!

8. Don't let the person make you mad or make you react. That is what the person using a bully action wants. Stay calm, ignore, walk away and tell someone.

9. Walk to school with someone.

10. Avoid kids who don't seem to like you or who are mean to you, and if possible, avoid places where they are.

11. Say something funny to show that you are not scared.

Help your child to understand that he can best combat bully actions by becoming confident and believing in himself—knowing who he is in his own self-concept—not accepting other people's negative labeling. Help your child to understand that learning how to be assertive can protect him from bully actions. There is no better self-esteem builder than having control over your life.

Let your child know that ignoring bully actions can be effective, although it may not work the first time it is tried. Teach your child not to give up on this idea.

If you see someone dealing with bully actions:

1. Be friends with that person.

2. Help the person tell an adult.

3. Don't join in when you see bully actions happening.

4. Stand up for someone else, but don't try to fight the person using bully actions yourself. Tell an adult or help your friend tell an adult.

Activities:

1. Read through the information in the protection lesson with your child and discuss.

2. Discuss the following questions with your child:

    - What types of bully actions do you see or experience?
    - Name some types of bully actions that you know about. Give some examples.
    - What victim responses encourage bully actions?
    - Why do people use bully actions?
    - Can one person use both bully actions and victim responses?

3. In response to bullying, together with your child, make a list of ways to:

    - ignore bully actions
    - minimize your reactions to bully actions

4. Discuss what each of you can do to prevent and stop bullying.

5. Use the following scenarios to discuss bullying situations with your child.

    a. **Jerry keeps on following Julia around the school.** He teases her about her long legs. Sometimes he tries to corner her alone and scares her. He has even kissed her. Julia is afraid of him. A few of her friends know that he is doing this, but she is afraid to tell anyone else. She is worried about really making him mad at her. No adults seem to be noticing that this is happening. Julia has stopped going to the cafeteria and has started staying in her classroom during lunchtime to avoid running into him.

Questions:
- Are these bully actions? Is this bullying? Does it fit with the definition of bullying?
- What can Julia do?
- What can her friends do?
- How do you think Julia might feel?
- How do you think Jerry might feel about what he is doing?
- What might happen to Jerry, if Julia and her friends get help?
- What might happen to Julia if she doesn't get help?

b. **A new girl, Sylvia, has recently arrived at school.** She is in a minority culture at school. Much of what she is experiencing is new to her. The most popular group in school decided that she is a loser and no one should be friends with her. The first month of school was terrible for Sylvia. She has had to deal with being called names and being pushed. Her books have even been wrecked. After about a month, she became friends with two girls she met in the library. Since then, the "most popular group" leave her alone a bit more.

Questions:
- Are these bully actions? Is this bullying? Does it fit the definition of bullying?
- How might this affect Sylvia?
- What can Sylvia do?
- How could the bystander students have stopped the bully actions?
- Why might the "most popular group" be using bully actions?

- Why have they eased up on their treatment of her?

c. **Benny is worried about going to school.** An older kid, James, is always punching his shoulders and pinching his arms and chest. James laughs when he does it. Benny has a whole bunch of bruises. James is bigger, so Benny just tries to laugh it off and pretend it doesn't hurt, but he is getting worried about going to school.

Questions:
- Are these bully actions? Is this bullying? Does it fit the definition of bullying?
- What can Benny do?
- How do you think Benny might feel?
- How do you think James might feel about his behavior?
- What could bystanders do?
- What might happen to James if Benny gets help?
- What might happen to James if Benny doesn't get help?
- What might happen to Benny if he doesn't get help?

d. Discuss bully actions and "bullies" found in modern media. This could be any characters that use aggressive behavior to get their own way. Discuss how we make these media characters into heroes and people to admire. Reality television shows can be included in this discussion as well.

Connect with **No Such Thing as a Bully** on social media and start a discussion about bullying in the media.

Protection Eleven: Saying No

GOAL: To become comfortable saying no.

Saying no is hard! It is one of the things that most of us find uncomfortable at one time or another. Sometimes it's just easier to say yes, to avoid the consequences. Have you ever said yes to your child in order to avoid the consequences of saying no? Most people have.

Part of standing up for yourself in the face of bully actions is learning to say no. Learn to say no to being treated badly; learn to say no to accepting the way other people are defining you; learn to say no to going along with bullying by others.

You need to know how to say no, in order for your child to learn how to say no. You need to respect yourself enough to say no when necessary. It might be no to overloading your schedule, or no to how someone treats you. Your child needs to see you controlling your own life, in order to learn that there are ways for them to control their own lives.

A key to saying no is the way the no is given. Often in the process of saying no, the other person is hurt. You might give the no too quickly, without tact, or you might impose a guilt feeling on them for asking. You might explain too much or too little, or you might, in a passive-aggressive manner, say no – by putting the other person off and not really giving him a clear answer in the end. People become angry because of their feelings, not because of the no. The trick is to learn how to say no respectfully, clearly and at the right times for you.

Here are some ideas for changing your perceptions about saying no:

- It is your right to meet your own needs by saying no. It is your responsibility to say no in a way that is timely and respectful.

- When you say no to one thing, you are making room for yourself to be able to say yes to something else that is important to you.

- Saying yes when you really want to say no will cause you to be resentful and angry about the request. Saying yes when you really mean no can ruin relationships.

- If you have been doing your share to keep a relationship going, and you are unable to grant a favor to the other person at this time, a clear explanation rather than avoidance or trickery is necessary.

- Have an open and honest look at your life as it is at present. Are you spending time on the things that you value the most? Is much of your time taken up with things that you don't value? Arrange your time so that the majority of it is spent doing things that match the values that you feel are important in your life.

- Following are some solid ideas for helping you to say no: When you say no to one request, look for something else that you can say yes about. If your child can have a treat later, tell them what time they can have it, instead of simply saying 'no'. If someone asks you to chair a meeting that you will be attending, decline respectfully and make an offer that you are willing to follow through on, such as bringing refreshments.

Don't answer right away; give yourself time to think about it. Phrases such as "I will check my schedule and get back to you," or "I need some time to think about that," are helpful. Get back to the person in a timely manner. You can even give the other person an idea of when you will be able to answer. "I can let you know next week." Then do it!

- Be clear when you say no. Don't use words such as "maybe" or "probably" when what you really mean is no. It is respectful to others to let them know where you stand. You can be clearer in saying no by being aware of your body language. Shake your head "no" and look the other person in the eye.

- Make a point of saying no to something every day, just for practice. Try it out on some telemarketers!

- If you must say no to someone who you would like to try to help, express that you would like to be able to help. "I can't do that tonight. I wish I could help. Please ask me another time."

- Express empathy to the person asking, so they feel understood. "I can understand why you need help with that. I bet it's a big job."

- Start off by saying no. It is easier to back up what you've already said than it is to try to get back to saying no after you've said a few sentences.

- Flip flopping your answer can often be confusing and difficult for people.

Go through the following ideas with your child at their level.

- Remember the Bill of Rights and Responsibilities: "You have the right to say no. You have the responsibility to say no clearly and respectfully."

- When you have to say no to one thing, you might be able to say yes to something else. "No, I can't come over today. How about tomorrow?"

- If you must say no, and you would still like to help, look for other ideas. "No you can't copy my homework. I'll help you with yours if you want."

- Say no and give a reason. "No, I don't like amusement park rides."

- Be clear when you want to say no. Don't say maybe or probably if you mean no. "No. I don't want to do that."

- Say no and add thank you. "No thank you."

- Change the subject.

    "Let's break this window."
    "No, let's go to my place and play video games."

- Keep on saying no.

    "Let's cut up these books."
    "No, that is wrong to do."
    "C'mon, Let's do it!"
    "No, that is wrong to do."
    "It will be fun!"
    "No, that is wrong to do."

- Use your smarts to stay away from trouble. If you know of places where there could be trouble stay away.

- Say no to bullying right when it starts by saying, "It is not okay for you to treat me that way." As a bystander say no to bullying by paying attention to how others are being treated. Stand up and say, "NO. It is not okay to treat them that way!"

- Use your body language to help you say no.

    "Let's hit that new kid!"
    "No," and walk away

Activities:

1. Practice saying no with your child. Stand in front of the mirror; stand up straight and say "NO". You can also use this time to talk about saying no to stranger danger and practice yelling really loud.

2. Start noticing how much you say "no" in a day, and how you say it. Talk about it during the day with your child.

3. Talk with your child about times when you both have to say yes.

4. Talk with your child about times when you both have to say no.

5. When you are watching television commercials, practice saying no to them.

Protection Twelve: "I" Sentences

GOAL: To learn to use "I" Sentences in difficult situations.

In order to teach "I" sentences to your child, you have to have a good understanding of them as well. Using "I" sentences can help to clarify thoughts and express your desire to deal with conflict in a positive manner. An "I" sentence is made of three parts.

1. "I feel _____."

    Starting off with your emotions about the situation puts the focus on the speaker. A sentence that begins with "You..." will most often be seen by the other person as blaming or accusing. Starting off a conversation by blaming someone puts up walls that make further positive discussion difficult. Starting off with emotion tells the other person that there are true effects of the situation that must be resolved.

    "I feel angry."
    "I feel anxious."
    "I feel stressed."

2. "When ..."
   "About the ..."
   "About my ..."

    The second part of an "I" sentence involves naming the action that distresses you. Be concrete and specific. Don't put in any assumptions. This must be factual, non-blaming and non-judgmental.

    "I feel angry when your tone of voice sounds angry to me."
    "I feel anxious when you stay out really late."
    "I feel stressed about my workload."

3. "Could we try...?"
   "I'd like to talk about it with you and see what we come up with."
   "What if we..."
   "I'd like to try..."

The third part of an "I" statement looks toward the future and suggests options for resolution. This will take many forms, but again works best if it remains non-blaming and non-judgmental. Who wants to work toward a solution when they feel judged and blamed?!

To put it all together then:

- "I feel angry when your tone of voice sounds angry to me. I would appreciate talking in a calm way."
- "I feel anxious about the report getting done on time. I'd like to discuss ways that we can be sure the work gets done."
- "I feel stressed about my workload. I'd like to talk about it with you and see what we come up with."

Plan ahead. In the beginning, using "I" sentences will feel awkward and new. It will be necessary to work at the phrasing and to think about what you are going to say. If all you can come up with is: "I feel angry when you breathe, could you please stop," you must work harder at identifying the specific issues!

Being assertive means choosing how to react; not just reacting. Taking the time to decide what you will say is choosing how you will react. These examples of "I" sentences show ways you can start off a difficult conversation. "I" sentences can also be used throughout a conversation in order to clearly express your feelings and wishes.

The following gives you other language to explain "I" sentences to your child:

1. An "I" sentence starts with "I" because then the focus is on you. They use feelings, because it's pretty hard to argue with feelings. If you say you are sad or angry, then no one can really argue with that. How you feel is how you feel.

    "I feel sad."
    "I feel sorry."

2. The middle part of an "I" sentence tells what is happening.
   - "I feel sad when I am hit."
   - "I feel sorry that I hit you."
3. The next sentence has answers to the problem.
   - "I feel sad when I am hit. Please don't hit me again."
   - "I feel sorry that I hit you. I won't hit you anymore."

A bystander can also use an "I" sentence. For example, "I am upset when I see people being mistreated. I need you to stop that." Parents can also use "I" sentences with their children. "I" sentences enhance relationships and understanding.

Activities:

1. Use the following scenarios to practice making "I" statements.
   - There is a girl that you only see in the hallways who comments on your clothes each day at school. You don't appreciate her commentaries. Use an "I" sentence to tell her how you feel and what you want her to do.

     (You are a bystander; how can you use an "I" sentence to intervene?)

   - A friend is pressuring you to have a cigarette and you don't want to. How can you say no, using an "I" sentence?

     (You are a bystander; how can you use an "I" sentence to intervene?)

   - You are standing in line at a drinking fountain and someone pushes ahead of you. What will you say? Use an "I" sentence.

     (You are a bystander; how can you use an "I" sentence to intervene?)

   - You are eating in the cafeteria and another student

comes in, threatens you and takes your lunch. Use an "I" sentence to the student.

(You are a bystander; how can you use an "I" sentence to intervene?)

- Your friend keeps on wanting to borrow money from you. He asks again and you can't lend him any more money until he has paid you what he owes you. Use an "I" sentence to tell him so.

- Your household chore is taking out the garbage and cleaning the bathroom. You hate these jobs. You would rather sweep the floor and vacuum the rugs. Use an "I" sentence to tell your mom or dad.

Notice that these are not all bullying situations—an "I" sentence is handy a lot of the time.

2. Use the scenarios above one at a time and answer the following questions:

- How would you handle it if you are assertive?

- How would you handle it if you are aggressive?

- How would you handle it if you are passive?

- How would you handle it if you are passive-aggressive?

3. Use "I" sentences in everyday life; notice out loud when you and your child are using them.

Protection Thirteen: Always and Never

GOAL: To notice and eliminate improper use of definitive language.

This is a short, self-explanatory protection lesson. When you use the words *always* and *never*, you escalate conflict and are generally communicating poorly. If you tell your child they *never* take the garbage out, they can think of the one time they did, and you are automatically wrong. Things are very rarely *always* or *never*, however when in conflict we often think they are. We believe we are *never* treated fairly, or that we *always* have to do more. Thinking *always* or *never* makes your emotional reactions stronger and can give the other guy a stronger fight, flight, or freeze reaction.

Sometimes people don't think they need to listen when they hear another person talking in extremes. It is better to put forward your case with facts.

Activities:

1. Talk with your child about the times you both use the words *always* and *never*.
2. Look for truths that really ARE *always* or *never*. For example, a lit match that is held to dry paper will always start a fire. Evaluate if your "truths" really are the truth, or if they need more detail.
3. During everyday living, watch for the use of the words *always* and *never* in your home.
4. Use the following paragraph to discuss which statements need more information to verify that *always* and *never* (and *every time*) is true. How can this be said in a way that would be more accurate?
   - "Jeff always hits me on the playground. Every time I go to the swings, he pushes me down and tells me that I can't use them. He never listens to me, and he always teases me."
   - "You never do what I ask you to do."
   - "You always call me names."
   - "You never clean up after yourself."

Protection Fourteen: Questions

GOALS: To understand questions and use them efficiently.

Knowing how to ask good questions facilitates friendships, introductions to groups and increases problem solving abilities. It's an important friendship skill, and of course, strong friendships are an important barrier to experiencing bully actions.

The difference between open and closed questions can be somewhat abstract, and it can be difficult to tell the difference. Questions can even be defensive, creating a fight, flight, or freeze response. How about when your child yells "Why do you hate me?"

Explain why this is important (as above) and review these ways of asking questions with your child. Different types of questions can be confusing but it is important to be able to tell the difference. There are closed questions and open questions. A closed question only asks for a little bit of information. It can be answered with a yes or a no, or sometimes by giving a little bit of information. Open questions require more information. Knowing how to ask open questions is an important part of getting to know someone else and understanding what the other person has said.

Some examples of closed questions:

- Are you all right? (yes or no)

- Is this the right way to do this? (yes or no)

- What is your address? (62 Bay Street)

- Where do you go to school? (Brighton School)

Some examples of open questions:
- What do you think?

- What interests you?

- What do you do for fun?

- Why is math your favorite subject in school?

Another type of question is the "defensive question." Defensive questions are often said with negative tone:

- "What are you doing here?"
- "Why are you doing that?"
- "Didn't you do that yet?"

Questions can change depending on how they are said. A question can sound nasty. Think about how a mom might say "Why aren't you home yet?" if a child was supposed to be home half an hour ago.

Activities:

1. Try playing a conversation game with your child, using only questions back and forth. No answers!

2. Brainstorm a list of questions together. Discuss each question. What are possible answers? Is it an open or closed question? Reinforce that it is often hard to tell!

3. Ask your child a question. Have him answer it, and then ask you a question. You answer it and ask another question, and so on, for as long as you choose.

Protection Fifteen: Tone of Voice

GOAL: To recognize and control different tones of voice.

Have you ever had a conversation with your child that went like this?

> You: Did you do your chores?
> Child: No (said with negative or angry tone).
> You: Please don't use that tone of voice with me.
> Child: I don't know what you are talking about.

Your child may or may not be aware of the tone of their voice. To give your child the benefit of the doubt, make them aware of the way tone can change the meaning of words.

Talk to your child from the point of view that we all have different tones of voice to use and that it is a perfectly natural thing. It is also a very positive thing to have control over when, where and how we use our tone. Tone is not only negative, although we tend to think of it that way. It is important for both you and your children to be sure that your tone reflects whatever it is that you intend to say. We've all been in a situation where our words come out distorted in some way or more angrily than intended.

In terms of preventing bully actions, being aware of tone, and being able to control it, assists in two ways. Awareness of tone is a friendship skill and can facilitate positive friendships, which prevents bullying. Control of tone, another friendship skill, can assist you in standing up for someone who is experiencing bully actions. Knowing how to sound firm can help to put off a person using bully actions.

Activities:

1. Using the phrase, "I didn't hit her," guide your child in an exercise where a stronger accent is placed on each indicated word. Both of you say the following sentences, with a stronger accent on the bold word.

    - *I* didn't hit her.
    - I *didn't* hit her.
    - I didn't *hit* her.
    - I didn't hit *her.*

Four statements, four distinct meanings. Discuss what each different sentence means. This is a quick way to show your child (and yourself!) that how words are said can change the meaning of a sentence.

2. Talk about the words and phrases that get thrown around when someone uses a negative tone. These might include lippy, smart aleck, smarty pants, "Don't use that tone with me." Let them know that using a negative tone is not the most effective way to get what they want. Discuss when tone has worked to get them what they wanted and when it has not worked. What kind of tones work? Which don't?

3. Talk with your child about the following:
    - What do you already know about tone of voice?
    - Does it sometimes work for you to have a rude tone of voice?
    - Do you get what you want?
    - Why does it work?
    - When does it not work?
    - Why doesn't it work?
    - What is a worst-case scenario for you about using a negative tone?
    - Are there situations where you are more likely to have a negative or positive tone in your voice?
    - Are there times when it seems like a good idea to have negative or positive tone in your voice?

    Brainstorm some other types of tone. (For example, excited or kind).

Protection Sixteen: Body Language

GOAL: To realize the effect of body language on bully actions by creating personal awareness.

Body language is amazing. If a child looks confident and appears as though they can take care of themselves, they will be less likely to be bullied. Both you and your children must be aware of what body language is saying.

You show people a lot of emotions that you don't intend to show them, whether you are aware of it or not. Sometimes you are angry and don't even know how angry you look or how angry your body language is. Other times you might be sad and not even know how sad your body language is. You might look vulnerable. Think about it:

When you are tired you might:

- Rub your eyes
- Put your head in your hands
- Close your eyes
- Yawn
- Stretch

When you are excited you might:

- Be shaky
- Be very active
- Hold your stomach
- Be jittery

When you are angry you might:

- Put your hands across your chest
- Frown, with your mouth and your forehead
- Shake your fist or stomp your foot

People use your body language to make opinions about you. Someone using bully actions might think you are a good target if he sees you walking with slumped shoulders and looking at the ground. If you look angry, people might be afraid to approach you.

Another part of body language is understanding body space.

- Intimate: 0 – 18 inches
- Personal 1.5 – 4 feet
- Social 4 – 10 feet
- Public 10 feet and beyond

Understanding body space allows your child to use space between himself and others appropriately, particularly if a child appears very shy or very aggressive.

Activities:

1. A body space exercise:
   - Stand 18 inches apart and throw a ball. This is intimate space. Discuss when it is appropriate to be this close to someone.
   - Stand 4 feet apart and throw a ball. This is personal space. Personal space is regular talking space. Discuss when it is appropriate to use this spacing.
   - Stand about 7 feet apart and throw a ball. This is social space. Social space is where you might stand if you have just met someone. Discuss when you might use this amount of space.
   - Stand 12 feet apart and throw a ball. This is public space. This is how much room you can give someone if you don't know them at all.

   Discuss what kind of spacing (generally public) is appropriate if someone is using bully actions against your child.

2. Have your child use the body language that goes with the descriptions above of tired, excited and angry.

3. Have your child practice standing up straight and looking confident. You can stand in front of the mirror with them and practice also.

4. Stand in front of each other and BE the mirror for your child. Have your child act out different body language types, and copy them, as though you are the mirror.

5. Talk about music and body language. What kind of body language is in music videos?

6. Watch some television shows together and talk about body language that you see.

7. For younger children, make up an action poem to recite. Simply brainstorm different actions – Hand on hips, arms across chest, arms out for a hug. String them together and say them, doing the action at the same time.

8. Have a box ready with the names of some emotions on slips of paper. Play charades using the body language that goes with the emotion.

Protection Seventeen: Thinking

GOAL: To examine how our thinking affects our behavior.

How we perceive our daily situations is often inaccurate and can make conflicts worse. When you are not thinking clearly, you can become more emotional. You feel more defensive and conflict escalates. The more extreme your thinking is, the more extreme your fight, flight, or freeze reaction will be as well. You can choose your thinking, and thus whether your reaction will be positive or negative.

We have a choice about how we are going to think. The exact same thing can happen to two different people, and they will react to it differently, depending on their thinking.

Imagine that two boys, at the same time, are asked to babysit. One boy thinks "Babysitting! That's for girls! I can't believe they asked me to babysit!" The other boy thinks "Babysitting! I haven't tried that before. It will be a good chance to try something and make some money." The first boy might spend some time being angry about how he was asked to babysit. He may not realize that times have changed and that boys care for children just as much as girls now. The second boy will have positive feelings. He will feel productive and capable.

Different thoughts + different feelings = different actions.

<u>Activities:</u>

1. Brainstorm situations where someone could react in a positive or negative way, depending on their thinking.

2. How can your thinking cause you to use a bully action?

3. How can your thinking cause you to use a victim response?

4. How can your thinking keep you from stepping up to help someone else who is being bullied?

5. Write down some of the thoughts you have when you see someone being bullied.

6. Write down some of the thoughts you have when you use a bully action.

Protection Eighteen: Inaccurate Thinking

Everyone thinks inaccurately at times. The first step to balanced thinking is gaining an understanding of how your thinking is inaccurate.

We all do it. Inaccurate thinking is unbalanced thinking. Not mentally-ill unbalanced, just an everyday, normal kind of unbalanced.

Inaccurate thinking is the kind of thinking that allows you to make assumptions about people: "Bill is just bad, all bad." It allows you to perceive situations as traumas: "This is the worst thing that could have happened." It allows you to feel that you have no control and that the currents of life just carry you wherever they choose, or it allows you to think that you do have control and can control others. Everyone experiences different levels and combinations of inaccurate thinking.

Inaccurate thinking doesn't take all the facts into consideration. It focuses on extremes – usually the extreme negative.

Inaccurate thinking is a habit that is developed over a period of years. If you really think about it, you probably learned your inaccurate thinking from a close role model. Did your mother tell you what you "should do," or "should have done"? Did your father talk about how politicians always lie, and pastors never do? Types of thinking are modeled for us. You pick up your own style of thinking along the way, based on your experiences and beliefs. You may believe stereotypes that make it easier to make assumptions about people. Assumptions about people will block communication and likely lead to conflict. You may have had experiences that lead you to believe that a certain type of person (male or female, Aboriginal or Caucasian, etc.) can't be trusted. Beliefs are the result of your experiences. Once you have a certain belief you tend to see the things that support that belief and ignore the things that don't. Changing beliefs is possible—not easy— but possible. The reason inaccurate thinking affects people so severely is because how you think about a situation will determine how you feel about it. You have emotions based on your thoughts. Some of your thoughts, you notice; some of them, you don't; and you react emotionally to most of them.

If you experience a great deal of inaccurate thinking, relationships may be affected. Knowing that your thoughts are inaccurate helps you to balance your thinking, which you will learn more about in the next protection lesson.

Here are talking points about inaccurate thinking and their associations to bullying:

Talking with Older Kids

Too controlling or not taking enough control: You can only control your own reactions. You do not control other people.

If you are experiencing bully actions, you may feel you have no control, which will lead to more helplessness. Knowing that you can control your own reactions can give you control over some of your situation. If you are using bully actions, you may feel you have some right to control other people. You don't. If you are a bystander you may think you have no control of the situation, but you do control how you respond.

Make me happy: Others cannot make us happy. You must make yourself happy with your own thinking and your own attitudes.

If you are experiencing bully actions, you may think they have to stop before you can be happy. This is false, you can still find happiness within yourself and the things you like to do. If you are using bully actions, you may escalate your use of them if people aren't making you happy. Remember that YOU are responsible for your own choices and happiness.

Overthinking Danger: Planning and dwelling on dangerous situations won't keep them from happening. Make your safety plan and then put it out of your head.

If you are experiencing bully actions, it is common to think about the danger a lot, and to feel anxious. Making a plan—and following it—can help with this anxiety.

Avoiding: Avoiding things that are making you anxious will only make you more anxious. You must face up to them.

If you are experiencing bully actions, tell someone and get some help in facing the problem!

Comparing: There is no sense comparing yourself to others. There will always be someone who measures up better or worse than you.

If you are using bully actions, you might compare yourself to others and lash out against those who you think are better or worse than you in some way.

Anger is just anger: Anger has an underlying emotion that sometimes feels "weaker." It might be sadness, or fear, but there is usually something under the anger.

If you are using bully actions or victim responses, you must understand and deal with the emotions that are underneath the anger you have.

Black and White Thinking: You consider yourself, other people or situations are all bad or all good.

If you are experiencing bully actions, you might look at other people and think they are only bad. If you are using bully actions, you might think the same thing. You need to know that everyone has good parts and bad parts to them. You must get to know them to find out more about them.

Negative Focus: Getting caught up in noticing only negative things about yourself, other people or situations.

If you are experiencing bully actions, you might believe a lot of negative things about yourself or others. If you are using bully actions, you might focus on the negatives in others to justify your own behavior.

Overgeneralizing: Thinking that uses exaggerated words like always, never and every time.

If you are experiencing bully actions, you need to be able to explain accurately what is happening so that people can understand.

Melodramatic Thinking: Everything is seen as a catastrophe!

Again, you need to be accurate in your thoughts and explanations about what you are experiencing. Very few things are true catastrophes!

Assumptions: You may assume things are true without having the facts.

When you are experiencing bully actions, you may begin to believe and associate things with it that are not true. These might be assumptions you have, and they could make the problem worse.

Mistakes mean that I am bad and don't know what I am doing: Mistakes are meant to be made and are meant to be learned from.

If you have used bully actions, you can understand that you've made mistakes, and can learn from them.

Everyone must like me: It's not possible for everyone to like everyone else.

If you are experiencing bully actions, remember that you don't have to keep friends that hurt you. Everyone is not going to like everyone else, even though we might still have to be in fairly close contact, as in school.

Should: The word should is usually used to make ourselves or other people feel guilty.

If you are experiencing bully actions, you might start to believe the hurtful things that are being said about you and be thinking, I should be thinner, smarter, or whatever. Should is an unhelpful word to use for yourself or others.

Talking with Younger Kids

In case your child is younger, these simpler definitions are also provided for your use. The above applications to bullying apply. It is not important that you and your child understand ALL of these. It is important that you gain the ability to pick out the types that you are using.

All good or all bad: We all have good and bad parts to us. Maybe you are a really good friend who gets a bit bossy sometimes. Or maybe your friend is usually kind, except when you want to share a certain thing that she has. Remember, no one is all good or all bad. We all have good and bad parts to us.

Anger is just anger: When we feel angry, we are usually feeling something else too. The something else is usually something like scared or hurt or sad.

The people around me must make me happy: Sometimes we feel like if everyone around us would give us what we want, we would be happy. Happiness doesn't come from getting everything you want. You can have all the latest toys and computer games and still not be happy. Happiness comes from inside and from the way you think about your life.

Mistakes are bad: Sometimes when we make a mistake, we feel like what we did was bad, therefore, we are bad. You are not bad because you make mistakes! Making mistakes happens because we are people. All people make mistakes. We can learn from our mistakes.

<u>**Activities:**</u>

Review the types of inaccurate thinking, using the following examples; also brainstorm other examples with your child.

Black and White	I hate you, mom! Steve is just all bad! I'm a total idiot!
Overgeneralizing	You never let me do anything! I have to do all the work in the house!
Melodramatic	This is the worst thing that could have happened!
Assumptions	I've never seen her go, but I know she's there all the time!
Control	I want you to do what I want to do! There is nothing I can do.
Should	I should be a better person. I should be able to do that.

Make me happy	If everyone would do what they should, I would be happy. I can't do anything that makes me happy.
Nobody likes me	I'm worthless because I'm not popular. I'm not in sports, so I'm a loser.
Mistakes are bad	I can't believe I said that out loud. What a loser! I'll never get this right!
Overthinking danger	I'm always worrying about getting hurt. Those thoughts are constantly in my head.
Comparisons	She's prettier than me. I'm ugly. He's better at sports than me. I'm weak.

Protection Nineteen: Automatic Thoughts

We send ourselves a lot of automatic thoughts each day. This is a phenomenon that occurs for everyone at some level. Your automatic thoughts are often connected to the types of inaccurate thinking you use. For example, if you tend to compare yourself to others negatively, your inaccurate thoughts may reflect that: "I'm so fat," "I'm so ugly."

Automatic thoughts take different forms for different people. Some may experience them as sentences flashing through their brain. Others may see pictures of past or anticipated events and situations. Some may experience memories of comments made about them personally. They may hear voices from conversations they have had in the past. Automatic thoughts may be thoughts that you have about yourself, or about what someone thinks of you. They may be thoughts about others, or about the world.

You don't always notice your automatic thoughts. They flash by so quickly that you are seldom aware of their content. Automatic thoughts are most often negative, and they are most often believed. Automatic thoughts will often remain completely unnoticed until you are encouraged to notice and evaluate them.

The examples are many and diverse. What they will be for you will depend on what your past experiences have been. Negative thoughts are most often linked to the forms of inaccurate thinking you use. Some of these might include:

- "I'm such a big loser."
- "No one would ever want to be with me."
- "I can't do anything right."
- "I'm no good at sports."
- "I'm fat."
- "I'm a bad parent."

Others might include memories of people making negative comments about you, or of times when you feel you have not been successful.

One example of automatic thoughts might be the rerun that happens in your head about a situation you've experienced. You may find yourself repeating the situation mentally, worrying about it, worrying what people might be saying or thinking about you. Another example of a situation involving automatic thoughts is the woman who feels great about herself in the morning, but by noon has decided that she is a fat slob. As it is unlikely that there was any great weight gain in the four hours from 8:00 a.m. to noon, it is likely that she has had automatic thoughts that have led her to an emotional reaction.

This brings us to the reason automatic thoughts can be so devastating. You react emotionally to your thoughts. If your thoughts are consistently negative about yourself, others and the world you will experience consistently negative emotions. This affects your self-concept. When it is negatively affected, you are at risk of accepting and integrating other people's negative opinions about you. In the context of bullying, when a child begins to accept negative opinions about themselves, integrating those thoughts and beliefs into their being, anger builds up and they are susceptible to turning it on themselves. They come to believe the negatives that others are handing them.

In order to prove or disprove automatic thoughts, they must be caught, noted and examined for evidence. Learning how to do a thought record will help you to do just that— catch the thought; remain aware of the thought, and examine it for supporting or contradicting evidence. Taking into consideration the positive, as well as, the negative aspects means a more balanced way of looking at self, others and the world.

Explain to your child:
You must do something with all those automatic thoughts you have. Learning balanced thinking techniques can help you to feel confident and sure of yourself.

When someone says something negative about you, you might begin to believe it. When you believe the negative messages about yourself, it shows, and it is hard to feel confident. If you believe you are a loser, or if you think you will never do anything right, you will have trouble standing up straight; talking to people. You'll have trouble in all sorts of ways.

The next lesson, Protection Twenty: Balanced Thinking covers important questions to ask yourself in order to balance out your automatic thoughts. It can be helpful to write out the answers to your balanced thinking questions. Whenever you have recurring thoughts, you can go back to those answers and they will remind you about how to deal with automatic thoughts.

In direct association to bullying, children taking on each of the three roles, might have the following automatic thoughts:

- **A child using bully actions:**

    They did it first, so it's okay.

    He's a loser anyway; he deserves it.

    I'm tough.

- **A child using victim responses:**

    What did I do to deserve this?

    I'm such a loser.

    I wish I had more friends.

- **A child who is a bystander:**

    There's nothing I can do.

    I'm glad that's not me.

    I am scared to do anything.

Activities:

1. Brainstorm automatic thoughts that you and your child use. Talk about how each of you feel when you have those thoughts.

2. Using the following role plays, take some guesses at what kind of automatic thoughts each person is having:

- Tammy and Julie used to be good friends but lately Julie is spending more time with Shelley. Tammy is angry and is yelling at Julie about it. Julie is yelling back.

- Billy keeps on bumping into Joey and hip checking him into the locker. Billy says it's no big deal and Joey can't take a joke when Joey tries to talk to him about it.

- Marnie and Olivia were good friends, but Olivia has been going to parties and drinking and Marnie doesn't want to be involved. Marnie and Olivia are both talking about each other in the hallways.

Go on to the next protection lesson to learn a balanced thinking tool.

Protection Twenty: Balanced Thinking

GOAL: To increase both parent and child's ability to use balanced thinking to combat negative or inaccurate thoughts.

Balanced thinking provides your child with an important tool that contributes to:

- problem-solving
- building positive relationships
- avoiding criminal and other negative activity
- avoiding and recovering from mental illness or anxiety
- managing conflict
- providing a strong basis for adult life.

In order to teach this to your child, you must learn it as well. Here is an example of a situation and a thought record from a parental perspective:

> Sue Ann has been worried about her relationship with her seventeen-year-old daughter, Carissa. Carissa has been pulling away from the family, spending more time with her friends than she does at home. She doesn't tolerate questioning about her activities very well, resulting in a lot of arguments. Last night she didn't come home at all. Sue Ann hasn't approached her about it yet. She fears that it will just lead to a blow up and Carissa will end up leaving. Sue Ann doesn't know if Carissa is using drugs, alcohol, or having sex, but these are certainly possibilities. Sue Ann doesn't know if she should push the situation further, let it go, or just what to do. Sue Ann is feeling very distressed and confused.

Sue Ann's Thought Record

Situation: Thinking about how to approach Carissa about staying out all night.

Emotions: fear, anxiety

Automatic Thoughts:

- She is going to get mad and leave.
- I'm going to yell my head off.
- This is going to ruin any future relationship between us.

Sue Ann picks the automatic thought that is the most distressing to her. She becomes very upset thinking about the future relationship between herself and her teenage daughter and how that relationship is going to be affected by all this fighting. She will focus on that automatic thought for the rest of the thought record.

Information that supports the automatic thought: This is going to ruin any future relationship between us.

- Carissa has walked out of the house before.
- We have been fighting a lot lately. We say hurtful things to each other.
- Carissa is getting older. She has older friends. She might just decide to move out.

Information that does not support the automatic thought: This is going to ruin any future relationship between us.

- Carissa has walked out of the house before, but she has always come back.
- Even if Carissa were to move out, it would not necessarily mean that our relationship would end.
- If I talk to Carissa respectfully and don't say those hurtful things, she responds better.
- Teenagers at age 17 tend toward pulling away from their families.

- Teenagers must be aware of the house rules and their boundaries.

A more balanced thought:

Although talking to Carissa about staying out all night may be difficult, it does not have to mean that our relationship will end. Carissa may be mad at me, but if I treat her respectfully things will be okay. If, and when Carissa does decide to move away from home, it does not have to mean that our relationship will end, just that it will change.

This can be repeated with the other automatic thoughts if they are also attached to strong emotions. This can also be repeated in many different situations. People often have the same repeated automatic messages—thought reruns. If thought records are kept, they can be re-used. When the thought rerun happens, the already-written thought record can serve as a quick reminder of a more balanced way to view the thought or situation.

Using the following questions, guide your child through the scenarios and help them think about the automatic thoughts in a balanced way.

Balanced Thinking Questions

- What is my automatic thought?
- What is true about the automatic thought?
- What is not true about the automatic thought?
- What is a different way to think about it?

1. Review the automatic thoughts that you previously brainstormed. Brainstorm the reasons that balanced thinking is important.

2. Using the following scenarios with your child, come up with some ways to apply balanced thinking. Some ideas are written in, but you and your child can brainstorm other automatic thoughts a person might have in the following situations and work through the questions.

Someone misses an important catch in a baseball game. His automatic thought: "I can't do anything right!"

- What is true about the automatic thought? "I just missed the catch."
- What is not true about the automatic thought? "There are other things that I do right. I have caught tough hits before. I have good marks in school."
- What is another way to think about it? "I do lots of things right. This time I missed the catch, that doesn't really mean that I can't do anything right."

Someone gets a poor mark on a test. Their automatic thought "I am stupid!"

- What is true about the automatic thought? "I just got a bad mark."
- What is not true about the automatic thought? "I am smart enough to have passed other tests. I didn't study hard enough for this one."
- What is another way to think about it? "I failed the test, but that doesn't mean I'm stupid. I've passed other tests and can learn from my mistake and study harder."

Someone gets bullied at school. Their automatic thought "This is my fault because I'm fat."

- What is true about the automatic thought? "I am overweight."
- What is not true about the automatic thought? "No one deserves to be treated badly no matter how they look."
- What is another way to think about it? "I can control my weight if I work at it. Other people being mean or rude is not my fault.

Someone sees another person getting bullied at school.

Their automatic thought "There is nothing I can do."

- What is true about the automatic thought? "It is a hard situation."

- What is not true about the automatic thought? "There are things that I can do."

- What is another way to think about it? "I am frightened, but I can make choices about what I am going to do. I can ask an adult for help."

Protection Twenty-One: The Anxiety Equation

GOAL: To learn an effective tool to manage anxieties relating to any issues.

Feeling anxious and distressed about events taking place in your life can cause a great deal of stress. Adults do not own the right to be anxious. Children are living in anxious times and are exposed to so much that causes anxiety these days. Talking to your child about anxieties is an important conversation to have.

The Anxiety Equation isn't made of numbers (Greenberger and Padesky). It looks like this:

$$\text{Anxiety} = \frac{\text{High Estimation of Danger}}{\text{Low Estimation of Coping Skills and Resources}}$$

Anxiety must have these elements: a high estimation of danger and a low estimation of your ability to cope with it.

So what does this mean? It means that when you feel anxious or scared, you will often be thinking that the danger is higher than it is. Think about the worst thing that could happen. Is it as bad as you thought?

Now think about the skills you have, to cope with the danger. When you are anxious, you usually think that you are not going to be able to cope! But you have a ton of coping skills. You can use balanced thinking; you can use problem solving; you can use brainstorming; you can ask for help; you can use your good communication skills; you can practice relaxing; you can get any help or information that you need.

Coping skills can be very simple:

- Being able to take time alone

- Being able to talk to friends

- Knowing what is relaxing for you

- Knowing how to brainstorm

These three questions help you to work through the anxiety equation:
1. What is the worst thing that can happen?
2. Is it as bad as you thought it would be?
3. What must you do to handle it?

Activities:
1. Use the following examples to work through the anxiety equation.

   Issue: Fear of not doing well in a sports event.
   (Overestimation of Danger)
   Answer the questions to assess **Real Danger**:
   - Is there a chance that I could be more afraid than I need to be?
   - What facts show that this is something that I do have to worry about?
   - What facts show that this is something that I don't have to worry about?

   What I must do:
   (Underestimation of Skills and Resources)
   - Be aware of my own abilities.
   - Know that this is a team sport and winning isn't just up to me.
   - Talk to the coach if I am unsure about what I am supposed to be doing or need more information.

   Issue: Worry that homework will not be complete
   (Overestimation of Danger)
   Answer the questions to assess **Real Danger**:
   - Is there a chance that I am more worried than I need to be?
   - What facts show that this is something that I do have to worry about?

- What facts show that this is something that I don't have to worry about?

What I must do:
(Underestimation of Skills and Resources)
- Make a plan to get the homework done.
- Schedule certain times during the day to do homework.
- Have a specific place where I like spending time doing homework.
- Ask my parents for help in making a plan.
- Ask my teacher, if I have questions about the homework.
- Ask a friend for help.

Issue: Fear that my friends won't like me if I don't do what they want.
(Overestimation of Danger)
Answer the questions to assess **Real Danger**:
- Is there a chance that I am more worried than I need to be?
- What facts show that this is something that I do have to worry about?
- What facts show that this is something that I don't have to worry about?

What I must do:
(Underestimation of Skills and Resources)
- Practice saying no with my friends.
- Know that if my friends are forcing me to do something I don't want to do, they are not good friends.
- Know that even if my friends decide to dump me, I can make other friends.

Issue: Fear about walking to school because of experiencing bully actions.

(Overestimation of Danger)
Answer the questions to assess **Real Danger:**
- Is there a chance that I am more worried than I need to be?
- What facts show that this is something that I do have to worry about?
- What facts show that this is something that I don't have to worry about?
- **What I must do:**
- (Underestimation of skills and resources)
- Tell an adult. Be clear about what is happening.
- Make a different plan for getting to school that is still convenient.
- Walk with a group.

2. Now brainstorm things that you and your child feel anxious about and work through the anxiety equation with them.

Protection Twenty-Two: Taking Care of Yourself

GOAL: To place importance on the need of self-care.

Your child needs to know that taking care of himself is important TO himself. It is done for his own well-being.

This is basically a quick health lesson, added in because in order to be bullyproof, you must be taking care of yourself. If a child is healthy, physically and emotionally, he is less likely to engage in bully actions or victim responses.

Help your child to understand not only what he has to do to take care of himself, but also why, in terms of himself and his own life.

Activities:

1. Wash yourself like you would in the shower, washing each part. Have your child mirror what you are doing as you do it.

2. Have a discussion with your child about personal care. Introduce a nutritional food guide and healthy diets. If you are not already eating according to a healthy food guide, share in making the change with your child.

3. Search online for health sleep meditations.

Protection Twenty-Three: Lucky or Unlucky

GOAL: To examine the idea that we can wait to decide if something is bad or good.

Your child needs to understand life in a holistic way. Children often see adults over-reacting to things that happen in their lives. A quick reaction is often unwarranted, and it is truly hard to know right away if something is bad or good. This is important when our children are going through hard times, because there is the desire to end the hard time for them. It's important to understand that out of bad things *come* good. Your child grows through every experience and MUST be involved in his own solutions.

To illustrate this point, here is an excerpt from my first book:

> There seems to be an instant human reaction to jump to quick conclusions about whether a situation is a blessing or a curse. The reality is that we may not know for quite some time if what has happened is negative or positive. Often, what initially seems to be a blessing has some negative consequences. What initially seems to be a tragedy or a trial will result in some positive consequences.
>
> There are situations in which you may not ever know if there were positives. When I am running late for unforeseen reasons, I try to remember that there may be some unknown reason that I am late. This train of thought always makes me think of an experience that my family and I had while on vacation. My family and I were visiting a friend. We were to leave to attend a wedding on that Saturday, and would be staying overnight. With several of us to get ready and packed, we were fairly rushed. We probably could have planned better. In fact, I'm sure we could have planned better! There was much hurrying and double-checking.
>
> Finally, we were ready to go. Everyone was organized, clean and looked great. We had a bit of time to spare and could have a fairly leisurely trip to the wedding, a trip that should take one and a half hours. We'd have a little time to visit before the wedding. Okay, let's go, hurry up. Ummm... but where are the keys?

We searched, everyone in the house searched. Very calmly I might add. We decided to believe that we were meant to slow down for some reason. We turned the house upside down. We unpacked the luggage we were leaving behind and packed it again. We unpacked the luggage we were taking along and packed it again. We realized that one set of keys were in the locked vehicle, but there was still no sign of the other set. Forty-five minutes later, after we'd called to let them know we'd be late, and as I was calling a locksmith, the keys were found under the corner of a mat. That area had been searched several times previously. We made it to the wedding just minutes before it started.

Were we fortunate, or unfortunate? Would something tragic have happened if we had kept on rushing? We'll never know. What we do know is that taking it easy, and not deciding something is terrible right off the bat, keeps emotions more balanced. Problem solving skills are enhanced, rather than being impaired by anger or other high emotion. Learning experiences are more easily identified when emotions are balanced. Coming into a wedding late isn't the end of your world, getting into a traffic accident on the way there may be. (Karius, 44 - 45)

It can also be explained like this:

You don't always know if you are lucky or unlucky as soon as something happens. The things that seem unlucky sometimes turn out to be very good. The things that seem lucky sometimes turn out to be very bad.

When something unlucky happens, it is important to wait a little bit in order to see if the results are good or bad.

Sometimes, instead of waiting, we get upset right away. Not now, but RIGHT NOW! This can end up making things worse. If you get a poor mark on a test and you immediately react in a negative way, you might not handle telling your parents very well. You might be so upset that you get angry with them and say something that you don't mean or that gets you into trouble. If you take the time to think about how you want to react instead of just getting angry, you will probably be able to resolve the problem in a more positive way. You will also be less likely to use bully actions if you think about how you want to react. You will also be able to handle bully actions against you better.

Activities:

1. Write the words "Lucky or unlucky" on a piece of paper and put it in a place where it can be seen. Go back to this idea when something bad happens.

2. Have your child teach this idea to another adult.

3. With your child, brainstorm some examples of where something seemed bad and turned out good or seemed good and turned out bad.

    If they are unable to come up with examples, here are some ideas:

    - Has your bicycle ever broken down, but it was close to your house and you could just walk home? And then your dad helped you fix it and you had a really good time together?

    - Have you ever received a present that you thought you didn't want, then it turned out that you liked it or found it useful?

Protection Twenty-Four: Control

GOAL: To understand what is in our control, and what is out of our control.

We spend a lot of time fighting against and being anxious or angry about things we don't control! This lesson is intended to remind you and your child that there are things we can control, and things we can't.
In my first book I wrote this about conflict resolution:

> We spend a lot of time fretting about people and situations over which we have no control. We don't control our friends, families or spouses. Control of our children is lost before they leave the womb.
> We can't influence others by trying to make them be or become someone who acts the way we want them to. The only thing we have control over is ourselves, and the only way we can influence the behavior of others is through our own behavior. When we change our reactions, it often causes a chain reaction that changes the way others relate to us.
> An action plan is a plan for change. Rather than spending a lot of time on an action plan that tries to control others, know what you control.
> Listing the things that concern you helps you to evaluate which of them you can control. Use the list to determine what you directly influence - your own behavior, your attitude, your ability to work hard toward achievements. Any items you can change yourself, are the items over which you have total control. There are other people and circumstances that you can influence with your own behavior, but over which you don't have total control. This might include family members, friends, co-workers or situations at work. Place your focus on the areas that you directly control (Karius, 57-58).

I control my actions.
- I can hit or not hit.
- I can yell or not yell.
- I can smoke or not smoke.
- I can drink alcohol or not drink alcohol.

I control my thoughts.
- I can look at the positive or the negative side of things.
- I can work to have balanced thinking.
- I can know that my automatic negative thoughts are not true.

I control my behaviors.
- I can be kind or mean.
- I can be respectful or disrespectful.
- I can be helpful or unhelpful.

I have no control over . . .
- other people.
- the weather.
- where or how my parents live.
- what my friends or siblings do.
- other people's schedules.
- other people's thoughts.

Activities:

1. Use the list above to talk about which things your child has control of, and which they do not. Discuss how they have control, what actions they could take and what impact their actions might have on different situations.
2. Make a "Things I have control of" list with your child.

Protection Twenty-Five: Affirmations

GOAL: To write and use affirmations to reach goals, counteract inaccurate thinking, and to balance thinking.

Back in the day, before we really knew how affirmations worked, a lot of people had negative experiences with them. I can remember being told to look in the mirror and tell myself "I love you." It made no sense to me. I never did it. It felt too ridiculous. The goal here is to have you understand the mechanics of using affirmations before you start. This will minimize any sense of ridiculousness that might exist about using the tool.

This protection lesson will focus on using affirmations in two ways:

1. Picture your goal. This could have to do with relationships, money, personal development, emotional states – any goal at all really! You can write affirmations that show you reaching the entire goal, or you might break the goal down into steps, and write affirmations about the steps.

2. Write down the negative thoughts you are having (inaccurate thinking), then write affirmations that are the opposite, or counteracting of the negative thought.

Through our experiences and lifestyle, we learn patterns—not only patterns of action, but also patterns of thought. These thought patterns become lodged in our subconscious, and our subconscious works to keep us thinking at the status quo to which we are accustomed.

Using affirmations affects the subconscious and begins to change that status quo pattern. To illustrate this, I'm going to use a story about one of my own affirmations. One of my historical actions is to be slow at putting things in snail mail. I have a series of thought patterns around this issue. "It's troublesome." "There are a lot of steps to this." And probably one that affects me the most, is that during a difficult time in my life, I would frequently get bad news by mail, which caused an increase in anxiety around issues relating to mail. "Mail makes me anxious." This culminates in one main thought. "I'm bad at putting things in the mail." When I write affirmations for the day, and I write, "I am excellent at putting things in the mail." I actually have that thought when I think about mail – and it results in actions that lead to, well, putting things in the mail.

The effects of affirmations are different than the effect of making a list. A list is a bunch of stuff that has to be done. An affirmation is the gas in your thought engine that leads to success in completing a list.

When you are using affirmations to complete a goal, they can be broken down into steps. Consider:
what part of reaching this goal is difficult? What do I tell myself about it? How is what I tell myself helpful? Harmful?

Let's say I want to run a 5K, but I'm starting from the point of out of shape. I break it down into the steps:

1. Get a check-up. Thoughts: I hate going to the doctor. What if something bad is found? Affirmation: I proactively take care of myself.

2. Get a gym membership Thoughts: I'm too out of shape to be in a gym. Affirmation: I deserve wellness.

3. Test my strength and stamina. Thoughts: I'm weak. Affirmation: I am good the way I am. I will grow stronger if I want.

The structure of affirmations is important. Make sure they contain the word "I". Let them describe what you want to move toward. Use present tense as though they are happening right now. Avoid words like can, will and should. Stick to words like am, do and have. They are action words.

You will see that you can create an affirmation for every step of the way, as needed. A strong personal affirmation reflects the negative thought of an individual, turning it into a positive.

Watch your thoughts for negative talk about yourself. "I am a loser" becomes "I am a winner." "I am uncoordinated" becomes "I am coordinated." "I am fat" becomes "I accept myself the way I am."

If any of those feel like too much to manage, for example, if the idea of accepting yourself the way you are feels impossible, or if you know that you have goals related to the thought, then you may need to break it down into the beliefs and thoughts that underlie the thought. You're just going to dig a little deeper into the things that affect that thought, nutrition, health, exercise, practice. This includes things related to basic lifestyle choices. You might create a series of positive affirmations that include; "I eat healthy foods." "I welcome exercise." "I create wellness." "I practice coordination." These action-oriented affirmations will paint a scenario in your mind about something that has not yet happened.

Activities:

1. Round up all your negative thoughts about yourself. Create affirmations that are the opposite of the negative thoughts.

2. Go to YouTube and search "Dr. Emoto Water Experiment." You will find videos of different lengths, from 3 minutes to an hour and a half. Pick a video and watch it together. The point is to see how water in your body is affected when you speak negatively to yourself.

3. Create three small jars of cooked rice all under the same conditions. Daily, speak positive words to one jar. Speak hate to another. Ignore one. See what happens to all three jars over a 6 to 8-week period. To see what to expect, go to YouTube and search "Rice Experiment."

4. Use children's crayons to write affirmations in the shower or bath while getting ready for the day or ending it.

5. Write affirmations on small pieces of paper and post them around your home.

Plans to Review

Develop a plan for using this material into the future. Keep this book at hand and review it periodically. The most effective way to incorporate these ideas into your life, and your child's life is to use them daily. Remember that keeping the lines of communication open with your child and teaching him to be a strong communicator is going to make him resistant to using bully actions or victim responses. Not only are you making your child resistant to these actions, you are also providing the strong communication and thinking skills that your child will need in order to maintain positive relationships throughout his life.

If you want further support, get in touch! **No Such Thing as a Bully** has a membership community ready for you to join and start implementing these ideas with extra support and year-round learning!

References

Canadian Public Health Association. (2004). *Assessment Toolkit for Bullying, Harassment, and Peer Relations at School.* https://www.cpha.ca/assessment-toolkit-bullying-harassment-and-peer-relations-school

CBC News. (April 18, 2002, 9:45 AM). "Emmet's parents speak out." https://www.cbc.ca/news/canada/nova-scotia/emmet-s-parents-speak-out-1.342868

Coloroso, Barbara. (2004). *The Bully, The Bullied and the Bystander.* HarperCollins Canada.

Cox, Kevin. (April 12, 2002) "Suicide boy told to pay or be beaten." https://www.theglobeandmail.com/news/national/suicide-boy-told-to-pay-or-be-beaten/article1022368/

Dana, Dr. Daniel. (2001). *Conflict Resolution: Mediation Tools for Everyday Worklife.* McGraw-Hill Education.

de Becker, Gavin. (1999). *Protecting the Gift: Keeping Children and Teenagers Safe (And Parents Sane).* Dell Publishing: New York, NY.

Goleman, Daniel. (1996). *Emotional Intelligence: Why it Can Matter More Than IQ.* Bantam Books: New York, NY.

Greenberger, Dennis and Padesky, Christine A. (1995). *Mind Over Mood – Change How You Feel By Changing the Way You Think.* The Guilford Press: New York, NY.

Karius, Kelly. (2004). *THIS IS OUT OF CONTROL! A Practical Guide to Managing Life's Conflicts.* Karius & Associates: Melville, SK.

Rigby, Ken. University of Australia. http://www.kenrigby.net/. Bullying definition adapted from Rigby and used by permission.

Rounthwaite, C. J., PCJ. (March 25, 2002). "Citation: REGINA v. D.W. and K.P.D." Provincial Court of British Columbia: Youth Division. http://www.theprovince.com/pdf/bullying_judgement.pdf

Shippey, Gordon. (May 9, 2011). "The Curious Case of Casey Heynes," *Counselling Resource*. https://counsellingresource.com/features/2011/05/09/curious-case-casey-heynes/

Contacts for No Such Thing as a Bully®

Email: kelly@nosuchthingasabully.com

Facebook: http://facebook.com/groups/nstaabchallenge

Phone: 403-447-4404

www.ingramcontent.com/pod-product-compliance
Lightning Source LLC
Chambersburg PA
CBHW072047290426
44110CB00014B/1579